MOBILE DATA
COMMUNICATIONS SYSTEMS

The Artech House Mobile Communications Series

John Walker, *Series Editor*

For a complete listing of *The Artech House Telecommunications Library,*
turn to the back of this book.

MOBILE DATA COMMUNICATIONS SYSTEMS

Peter Wong
David Britland

Artech House
Boston • London

Library of Congress Cataloging-in-Publication Data

Wong, Peter, 1969–
   Mobile data communications systems / Peter Wong and David Britland.
      p.   cm.
   ISBN 0-89006-751-1 (acid-free)
      1. Mobile communications systems.   2. Wireless communication systems.
   I. Britland, David.   II. Title.
   TK6570.M6W66   1995   95-4987
   004.6'5—dc20   CIP

British Library Cataloging in Publication Data

Wong, Peter
Mobile Data Communications Systems
I. Title   II. Britland, David
621.382

ISBN 0-89006-751-1

© 1995 ARTECH HOUSE, INC.
685 Canton Street
Norwood, MA 02062

International Standard Book Number: 0-89006-751-1
Library of Congress Catalog Card Number: 95-4987

10 9 8 7 6 5 4 3 2

▼▼▼

CONTENTS

▼▼▼

PREFACE

Mobile data communications is still a new subject. As the mobile communications industry is heading towards an explosion in data communications, it seems appropriate that a book should cover the concepts behind this potential market. This book takes the reader through the principles behind mobile data communication system design. The book also introduces, in detail, the current and future wireless network and systems standards that support data communications and discusses the network architectures and applications. With an increasing emphasis on open standards, the book is timely as it introduces new mobile data communications standards being developed in Europe, the U.S., and elsewhere. Current and future systems standards that have data communications capabilities are reviewed.

The principles of mobile data communications are introduced in a different way from the traditional methods used in classical cellular communications books. These are often highly analytical and require the reader to have some firm grounding in mathematics. Instead, this book introduces the subject from a conceptual standpoint and should appeal to a wider audience. Concepts are brought forward in a simple-to-understand manner, with minimal mathematics, and address the needs of readers from sales and marketing background as well as those of undergraduate and graduate students. For the serious student, a comprehensive list of references of the papers and standards from which the concepts are derived are included.

▼▼▼

ACKNOWLEDGMENTS

This book is made possible through the advice, encouragement, and contributions of both colleagues and friends from British Telecom Laboratories, University College of Swansea, Technical University of Vienna, Hong Kong University of Science and Technology, and AT&T—in particular, Sarah Dicks, Fred Halsall, Alberto Lasa, John Davis, Gerhard Schultes, Ross Murch, Justin Chuang and Anna Ip. I also wish to acknowledge the permission granted by McGraw Hill and the IEEE for publishing certain tables and figures.

Peter Wong

I wish to thank my colleagues at RAM for their help in checking some of the historical facts associated with the evolution of the mobile data market place. In particular, I would like to express my thanks to my long-suffering wife for her understanding during the writing of this book.

David Britland

Finally, we wish to thank our families, who have been extremely supportive throughout the effort in bringing this book together.

CHAPTER 1
▼▼▼

INTRODUCTION TO MOBILE DATA COMMUNICATIONS

Traditionally, data communications have been confined to transmission over the wireline network; however, with recent advances in radio communications, we have seen a rapidly growing interest in mobile or wireless data communications. An increasing number of people are beginning to experience the convenience and power of mobile data, and we should expect to see a large growth in this sector of the telecommunications industry in the very near future. Users of mobile data will expect to see a new wave of communications applications that will revolutionize the lives of users. For organizations, converting to mobile data would enable operations to be more efficient and productive.

This book will introduce the concept of mobile data, highlighting the different systems and related issues, and discuss the future of the industry.

1.1 EVOLUTION OF MOBILE DATA

The concept of mobile data dates as far back as the radio telegraph, when special codes representing alphanumeric characters were transmitted over the radio waves. The idea behind this has extended to transmitting data over analog radio networks. Initially, using voiceband modems with speeds up to 300 bits per second (bps), data were successfully transmitted over the first radio networks. With advanced modem technology, data transmission over first-generation analog cellular networks are now able to achieve speeds up to 14.4 kilobits per second (Kbps). With the first-generation analog networks, data transmission was only an option; however, second- and third-generation digital cellular radio networks have data communications capability as a standard feature. This clearly illustrates the importance of mobile data. Radio communication networks being developed are required to have data communication capability built in.

Along with data transmission over analog radio and cellular networks, we also saw the evolution of mobile data-only networks, specifically to address data users. These networks were developed with proprietary modems and access techniques and are still very much operating. However, with the development of newer standards, these networks will face competition from open standards, such as the cellular digital packet data (CDPD) standard.

In addition to the low bit-rate data such as that used over mobile radio and cellular networks, higher bit-rate wireless connections (through spectrum allocations) have been able to replace fixed wire LAN connections. Known as wireless LANs, the first modems were capable of achieving hundreds of Kbps. With advanced radio-access technology, these modems are now able to support high bit-rate data transmission, in the region of megabits per second (Mbps), approaching actual fixed wire LAN speeds. In the not-too-distant future, we will see multimegabit connections offering broadband integrated communications over the radio link.

1.2 MOBILE DATA APPLICATIONS AND SCENARIOS

Unlike voice communications, which have a limited set of applications, data communications overcome all of the limitations that voice experiences. With voice communications, information can often be misunderstood due to noisy environments or differing accents. As a result, conveying any information may take several minutes. With data, human interaction (and possible error) is constrained to request/response-type communications. With advanced error-control techniques available, data transmission has a very low probability of error. As a result, the time to convey a piece of information using data is often only a fraction of the time used by voice. Hence, using data is not only more accurate and efficient in relaying information, but this method provides savings in air-time cost as well.

Because of its efficiency, mobile data has been adopted in many environments. In some cases, it has phased out voice communications completely. Primarily in dispatch-type applications, where precise instructions must be conveyed with minimum delay, data is an obvious advantage over voice. As a result, this application scenario has been adopted in courier companies, taxi dispatches, and transportation companies for truck/fleet management.

Another major application area is in information or database retrieval. This is particularly useful when access to specific records are required; for example, in the medical field, ambulances equipped with mobile data are able to access patients' records. During emergencies, on the way to the hospital, patients' conditions can be relayed back to the hospital in preparation for the emergency. Using the same idea of application, police vehicles armed with mobile data capability are able to look up vehicle registration details or criminal records. In the commercial area, for example, mobile data enables field sales or support personnel requiring pricing information at customer's premises to communicate with the central database for specific records. Similarly, with traveling personnel, access to electronic mail is often important in keeping current with business updates. Mobile staff will no longer be required to search for a telephone socket—with a radio modem, access to mail or network databases can be gained immediately.

Other applications expected to capture the market include point-of-sale credit card transactions. Point-of-sale terminals can be mobile, and, when incorporated with inventory terminals, sales staff are able to perform a number of transactions, from looking up item prices to making sales. This frees up cash registers and increases the efficiency of sales staff.

Another application scenario is in telemetry. With remote sensors, data can be relayed via radio to operations and maintenance platforms. An example may be the maintenance of vending machines or telephones. Similarly, telemetry data can be sent to remote locations to monitor or switch equipment.

So far, we have outlined some of the typical application scenarios possible in the outdoor environment. However, mobile data applies indoors as well. With high bit-rate mobile or wireless data communications, the concept of the wireless office approaches reality through wireless LANs. The messy wired connections with conventional wired LANs can be uprooted, freeing all personnel from being confined to the desk. When an office reorganizes, there will be no need for rerouting of wires and cables. Furthermore, with wireless LANs, during business meetings, executives need not be burdened with remembering to bring documents or files, as they can be retrieved via wireless connections into the LAN. Such convenience will greatly aid and enhance the jobs of professionals.

The applications mentioned so far are just a small fraction of the applications possible. With ever-advancing technology in communications, we can expect to see enhanced services such as mobile videotelephones, intelligent vehicle navigation systems, and teleshopping. All of these will be detailed further in Chapter 11.

1.3 OVERVIEW AND SCOPE OF THE BOOK

The objective of this book is to reveal the concepts behind mobile data communications, highlighting system-design issues and treating the subject from a standards perspective. All of the current mobile and wireless communications standards are addressed, paying particular attention to the data capabilities of the system. However, in order for the reader to appreciate mobile data communications and capabilities, several tutorial chapters are introduced, describing the different modulation techniques, the mobile radio propagation environment and its consequences, and techniques that can be used to guarantee data integrity.

In Chapter 2, basic principles of analog modulation techniques are first addressed, leading into more efficient digital modulation techniques. The spectral efficiency of the modulation techniques are also discussed, with some practical considerations, such as power efficiency and implementation issues.

Chapter 3 walks through the mobile radio propagation environment, the characteristics of fading, delay and Doppler spreads, and the effect of such transmission impairments on the bit error rates (BER). A tutorial chapter, it tackles the complex issues from a conceptual standpoint rather than presenting a traditional treatment with mathematical models. However, for completeness, a detailed list of references from classical papers are provided.

As a follow up, Chapter 4 attempts to mitigate the negative aspects of mobile radio communications by introducing error-control techniques. Again, error-control concepts are used, rather than mathematics, and the different techniques such as forward error correction (FEC) and automatic repeat requests (ARQ) are addressed. Finally, implementation and choice of error-control techniques are discussed to enable the reader to appreciate the design of a mobile data network.

Wide-area data transmission over radio started in private mobile radio, and in Chapter 5, a look is taken at the past, current, and future standards in this field. In particular, the developing TETRA and DSRR standards are reviewed. Throughout the world, there has been an explosion in the use of cellular radio telephones. This has allowed the general public, as opposed to the professional user, to have access to mobile communications and with it the possibility of mobile data access. Chapter 6 reviews the data facilities available on the current analog networks, the data overlay networks, and the digital GSM network. The latter system offers a multitude of possibilities for voice and data transmission, together with gateway access into most fixed infrastructure networks, such as the PSTN, ISDN, and PSPDN.

In Chapter 7, four of the current mobile data-specific network designs are reviewed, and the advantages and disadvantages of the methods chosen by the various designers are discussed.

Chapter 8 talks about data transmission over cordless networks standardized in Europe and accepted internationally, such as CT2 and Digital European Cordless Telecommunications (DECT). Issues such as network design and the use of such systems for data transmission (both low and medium bit rate) are also addressed. The performance of such networks is also covered, as well as their suitability to provide a wireless data service in addition to the wireless PABX function that they primarily serve.

In Chapter 9, wireless LANs are discussed, along with the different technologies and the advantages/disadvantages of each of the techniques. Wireless LAN network design issues are also addressed, touching on mobility management and performance. In addition to wireless LANs, wireless bridges for internetworking are also included and discussed. Finally, the chapter concludes with wireless LAN standards and future wireless LAN networks.

Chapter 10 looks at the applications that have evolved for use over mobile data networks from the very early *function-specific* applications, such as data collection from vehicles, to the very complex AVL, command, and control now used by sophisticated transport operators. As the use of mobile data extends further into the public domain, these early *vertical* applications are now being complemented by *horizontal* ones such as e-mail and EDI.

In Chapter 11, we have a preview of the future, looking at prospective systems, the types of services that have been specified, and the applications that we can expect. Next-generation mobile data systems will revolutionize our lives with personal communicators, enabling us to talk, send and receive mail, shop, and access a wealth of information ubiquitously. The chapter also looks at the developing third-generation systems and the standards, in anticipation of the future.

CHAPTER 2

▼▼▼

MODULATION TECHNIQUES FOR THE RADIO CHANNEL

When transmitting digital data over a bandpass channel (the transmission channel is often viewed as a bandpass filter), the data stream must be modulated onto a carrier wave (usually sinusoidal). Data originate from a computer terminal, and the channel may be a radio link or fixed-wire telephone line. The modulation involves switching or keying the amplitude, frequency, or phase of the carrier in accordance with the data stream. When the information is encoded into the amplitude of the carrier, the technique is known as amplitude shift keying (ASK); when the information is encoded into the frequency of the carrier, the technique is known as frequency shift keying (FSK); and when the data stream is contained in the phase of the carrier, the modulation scheme is known as phase shift keying (PSK) [1]. The above techniques are the basic digital modulation schemes. From these three basic techniques, more complex hybrids of digital modulation can be developed for higher bandwidth efficiency and will be described in the following sections. The chapter will briefly cover some of the different modulation techniques available and will highlight some of the key issues in the choice of modulation schemes for data transmission in the radio channel.

2.1 FUNDAMENTALS OF DIGITAL MODULATION TECHNIQUES

Bandpass modulation can be defined as the process whereby the amplitude, frequency, or phase of an RF carrier is varied in accordance with the information to be transmitted. The carrier wave can take on the general form:

$$s(t) = A(t) \cos\theta(t)$$

where $A(t)$ is the time varying amplitude and $\theta(t)$ is the time-varying angle.
   The angle can be rewritten as

$$\theta(t) = \omega_0 t + \varphi(t)$$

where ω_0 is the radian frequency of the carrier and $\varphi(t)$ is the phase. The carrier wave can therefore be rewritten as

$$s(t) = A(t) \cos[\omega_0 t + \varphi(t)]$$

   The radian frequency ω, which takes on the units radians per second, can also be represented in Hz. Denoted by f, the two parameters are related by the relationship $\omega = 2\pi f$.
   Basic modulation/demodulation (modem) techniques require the transmitter to modulate the data and the receiver to demodulate the information stream received. Demodulation at the receiver can use either coherent or noncoherent detection techniques. In digital communications, the terms demodulation and detection are used together very often. Demodulation is the process by which the carrier is removed, and detection is the process of symbol decision. When the receiver uses the carrier's phase to detect the signals, the process is known as coherent detection. The receiver has knowledge of the carrier wave's phase reference, and we say that the receiver is phase locked to the transmitter. This is often achieved with a phase locked loop (PLL) at the receiver circuitry. Coherent detection is performed by cross correlating the received signals with the replicas generated at the receiver and making a decision based on comparisons with a threshold. In noncoherent detection techniques, the receiver does not utilize any phase-reference information. Noncoherent detection techniques have reduced complexity at the receiver, but at the expense of inferior performance compared with the coherent system.
   Table 2.1 shows some of the more general modem schemes [2].

TABLE 2.1

Coherent and Noncoherent Modulation Schemes

Coherent	*Noncoherent*
Phase shift keying (PSK)	FSK
Frequency shift keying (FSK)	ASK
Amplitude shift keying (ASK)	Differential PSK (DPSK)
Continuous phase modulation (CPM)	CPM
Hybrids	Hybrids

2.2 PROPERTIES OF DIGITAL MODULATION TECHNIQUES

Digital modulation techniques modify a carrier's amplitude and/or phase (and frequency, since phase and frequency are related). As such, digital modulation techniques are often described in terms of a vector. In vector notation, the phase and amplitude of the RF carrier are represented by a vector whose angle from the reference is the phase of the carrier and whose length denotes the amplitude of the carrier. The carrier can therefore be described in polar notation as a vector of length M and angle θ; together the signal is represented by $M\angle\theta$. In rectangular coordinates, the I and Q scales are used where the axes are in quadrature. The digitally modulated signal is often split into two branches—I is the inphase branch and Q is the branch in quadrature (90°) or out of phase. The I-Q diagram is often used to study the signal constellation points (or possible states). Figure 2.1 illustrates the digital I-Q modulation representation.

In rectangular notation, the phase is given by phase = arctan (Q/I) and the magnitude $M = (I^2 + Q^2)^{1/2}$. To convert from the polar representation to I-Q, the following relationship can be used:

$$I = M \cos\theta \text{ and } Q = M \sin\theta$$

2.3 SOME BASIC DIGITAL MODULATION TECHNIQUES

Having gone through the principles of digital modulation, we are now in a position to consider some of the basic digital modulation schemes. In this section, we will consider the binary PSK (BPSK), quadrature PSK (QPSK), and the minimum shift keying (MSK) techniques.

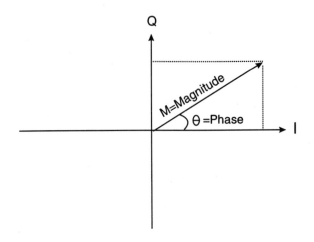

FIGURE 2.1 Digital I-Q modulation representation.

2.3.1 Binary Phase Shift Keying

BPSK is one of the simplest forms of digital modulation and is widely used in satellite communications systems. In BPSK, the phases of the carrier at binary one and zero are set 180° apart; i.e., the phase of the carrier is set to 0° when a binary one is applied to the modulator, and the phase is set to 180° when a binary zero is sent to the modulator. Figure 2.2 illustrates the BPSK signal. When viewed on the I-Q plane, BPSK appears as two points that are 180° apart on the I axis.

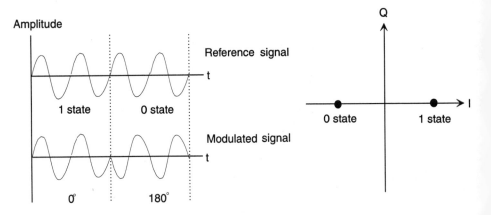

FIGURE 2.2 The binary phase shift keying signal.

Although BPSK is simple to implement, it is inefficient in its usage of bandwidth, which is essential in radio communications. As a result, BPSK is not widely used in land mobile radio applications. However, it is the most robust of all digital modulation techniques in the presence of multipath propagation effects (described in the following chapter) in the radio channel [3].

2.3.2 Quadrature Phase Shift Keying

QPSK (also known as four-phase PSK or 4-ary PSK) is a derivative of BPSK and a more complex digital modulation scheme. It uses four phase states, rather than the two used in BPSK, to represent the modulating digital data. It is used extensively in operational satellite communications systems. Viewed on the I-Q diagram, QPSK appears as four equally spaced points separated by 90°. Because QPSK has 4 possible carrier phase states, it is possible to have each phase state represent two bits of data, i.e., 2 bits encoded into one symbol. A term commonly used with bit rate is the symbol rate, which is often defined as the bit rate divided by the number of bits per symbol. For QPSK there are two data bits per symbol.

In the I-Q diagram in figure 2.3, we see the modulated QPSK at the four distinct phases of $\pi/4$, $3\pi/4$, $5\pi/4$, and $7\pi/4$, each representing one symbol containing two bits of information.

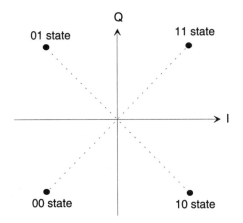

FIGURE 2.3 I-Q diagram for QPSK signal.

Because the symbol rate is half the bit rate, more information can be carried in the same amount of bandwidth. The spectral efficiency of a modulation scheme is often defined as the ratio of the bit rate to bandwidth, f_b/B, expressed in bps/Hz. The theoretical spectral efficiency of QPSK is 2 bps/Hz; however, to allow for practical filtering, an efficiency of 1.4 bps/Hz can be achieved.

A conventional QPSK modulator and demodulator is shown in Figure 2.4a. At the modulator, the incoming data stream is converted (by a serial to parallel converter) into the inphase and quadrature branches, each having a symbol rate of $f_s = F_b/2$.

The signals are then filtered and modulated by the inphase and quadrature carriers using the double sideband suppressed carrier amplitude modulation scheme (DSB-SC-AM) and combined to give a QPSK signal. The output is often filtered by a band pass filter (BPF) to limit its power spectrum, to prevent spill over into adjacent channels and to remove out of band spurious signals caused by the modulation process.

At the receiver, as shown in Figure 2.4b, the signal received is first filtered to remove adjacent channel interference and out-of-band noise. The signal at the filter output is split into two parts, each coherently demodulated (with the aid of the carrier recovery circuit, usually a Costas Loop) with the inphase and quadrature carriers [4]. The outputs are then lowpass filtered and, with the aid of the symbol timing/clock recovery circuit, the inphase and quadrature baseband signals are regenerated. The signals from the two branches are then recombined in a parallel-to-serial converter to produce the original bit stream.

2.3.3 Minimum Shift Keying

MSK is a special form of the frequency shift keying (FSK) technique. Like BPSK, simple FSK involves shifting the carrier between two values, using frequency instead of phase. [5,6]. MSK is a special case of FSK, with a modulation index of 0.5. It is known as MSK because the frequency spacing between the two frequency states (for 1 and 0 or *mark* and *space*) is the minimum spacing that allows the two frequency states to be orthogonal to one another. On the I-Q diagram shown in Figure 2.5, MSK appears to be a circle of radius one. Because the two frequency states are orthogonal, the shift in frequency translates to either a +90° phase shift or −90° phase shift (for either a one or zero data bit input into the modulator). On the amplitude versus time graph, MSK produces one cycle in the lower frequency shift and one and one-half cycles in the higher frequency shift for each data bit modulated.

The main advantage of MSK is that it is spectrally efficient with a faster roll off (more than QPSK [2]) and easily generated. When used with a premodulation Gaussian low pass filter (LPF), the modified technique is known as Gaussian minimum shift keying (GMSK) [7]. It is a very popular modulation currently in use in second-generation cellular and cordless systems.

2.4 MORE COMPLEX MODULATION TECHNIQUES

From the basic modulation techniques, we are now in a position to consider more popular methods currently in use in digital communications systems.

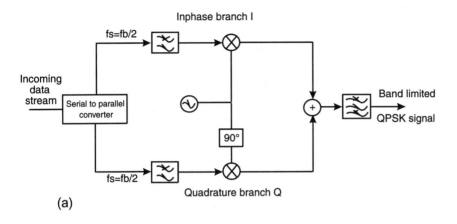

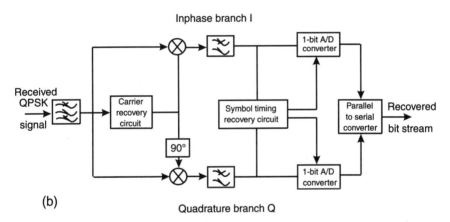

FIGURE 2.4 (a) A conventional QPSK modulator, and (b) a coherent QPSK demodulator.

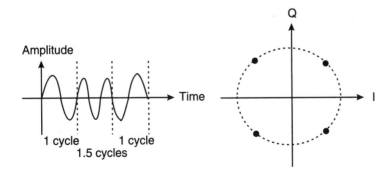

FIGURE 2.5 I-Q diagram for MSK.

2.4.1 Gaussian Minimum Shift Keying (GMSK)

As described in the previous section, when MSK is used in conjunction with a Gaussian LPF, the modulation scheme is Gaussian minimum shift keying or GMSK. Premodulation filtering is used to increase the spectral efficiency with sharper cut-off. Gaussian filters are maximally linear phase filters, which make them almost transparent to the transmitted data. At the same time, they provide enough filtering to allow fairly high spectral efficiency.

A GMSK modulator can easily be realized with a voltage-controlled oscillator (VCO) used with a premodulation Gaussian-shaped LPF, as shown in Figure 2.6a.

However, with the implementation shown in the figure, the VCO suffers from difficulty in maintaining the center frequency accurately within an acceptable range. With a phase locked loop (PLL) type modulator, this limitation can be overcome, as illustrated in Figure 2.6b.

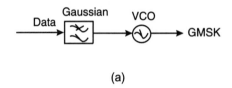

(a)

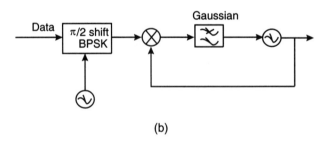

(b)

FIGURE 2.6 (a) VCO-type generation of GMSK, and (b) PLL-type generation of GMSK.

GMSK modulation has been employed in several communications systems. In the GSM digital cellular system, GMSK uses a BT product of 0.3. (B is the 3 dB bandwidth of the filter and T is the bit period. BT is often known as the bandwidth bit period product). GMSK is also used in the DECT system for integrated cordless communications (with a BT of 0.5) and in the RAM Mobile Data network; the Mobitex modem (by Ericsson) uses a BT of 0.3.

Although a lower BT has a higher spectral efficiency, it is more susceptible to errors. Therefore, a compromise must always be reached. The modulation efficiency of GSM is 1.35 bps/Hz (from a data stream of 270 Kbps on a 200-kHz channel). DECT, on the other hand, has a bandwidth efficiency of 0.67 bps/Hz (from a data rate of 1.152 Mbps in a 1.728-MHz channel)—the inefficiency is due to a large guard time to allow for intersymbol interference effects, as described in the following chapter.

2.4.2 $\pi/4$-Shifted QPSK

The $\pi/4$-QPSK modulation scheme is another very popular modem in second-generation wireless information networks. A variation of QPSK, it has carrier-phase transitions, which are restricted to $\pm\pi/4$ and $\pm3\pi/4$. The technique permits coherent as well as noncoherent demodulation. Noncoherent demodulation, as mentioned previously, enables simpler receiver structures than coherent demodulation techniques.

In a $\pi/4$-QPSK modulator, signaling elements of the modulated signal are selected in turn from two QPSK constellations, which are shifted by $\pi/4$ with respect to each other, as shown in the I-Q plot in Figure 2.7

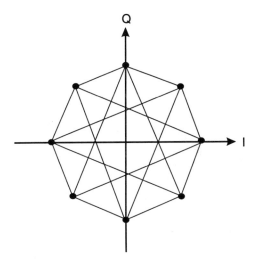

FIGURE 2.7 I-Q plot of $\pi/4$-QPSK modulation.

$\pi/4$-QPSK modulation and demodulation techniques are detailed in [8]. The technique has been adopted in the North American Digital Cellular (NADC) system, IS-54 and the Japanese Digital Cellular (JDC) system. In the NADC system, with a burst transmit rate of 48.6 Kbps through a 30-kHz channel, a spectral efficiency of 1.62 bps/Hz can be achieved, a 20% improvement in spectral efficiency over GSM. In the JDC system, with the channel bit rate of 42 Kbps over a 25-kHz channel, an even higher channel efficiency can be achieved, 1.68 bps/Hz [9]. In addition to cellular systems, $\pi/4$-QPSK is also being deployed in the European TETRA (Trans-European trunked radio) standard (with a modulation efficiency of 1.44 bps/Hz, from a gross data rate of 36 Kbps on a 25-kHz channel), which will be described for data transmission in the later chapters of this book. The Japanese digital cordless standard, personal handy phone (PHP) is also using $\pi/4$-QPSK for its modulation scheme.

2.4.3   Quadrature Amplitude Modulation

Another modulation technique widely used in digital microwave radio links is quadrature amplitude modulation (QAM) [10,11]. It is an attractive modulation scheme because it is multilevel and, hence, spectrally efficient. With the congested frequency spectrum, QAM is a good candidate for land mobile radio systems.

QAM, as the name implies, involves amplitude modulation on both quadrature carriers. It can take on any number of discrete digital levels, although the most efficient modulation schemes involve the number of levels to be equal to 2^n, where n is an integer. The basic QAM (n = 2) system is similar to QPSK, with the same constellation points in the I-Q diagram. The method of generating QAM is also similar to that for QPSK (as shown in Figure 2.4), with an option of the BPF after the summation of the I and Q signals. In QPSK, the BPF is often used for post-modulation filtering to maintain a constant envelope in the modulated waveform and is not required for QAM.

QAM techniques have the ability to take on many more states to increase the spectrum efficiency of the modulation technique. In the m-level QAM system, the I-Q diagram would consist of a square lattice of M points. An example of 16 QAM is shown in Figure 2.8. Although such modulation schemes are spectrally efficient, they are not power efficient and are more susceptible to errors, due to problems in the decision-making process at the threshold levels. One example is when a signal is in a fade.

QAM techniques have been proposed for use in future mobile radio communications systems [12], due to congestion in the radio spectrum. Known as variable-rate QAM, the scheme has been suggested as a method of increasing modulation efficiency at the cost of increasing complexity in the modems.

2.5   CHOICE OF MODULATION SCHEMES

We have discussed several different types of modulation schemes. However, it is beyond the scope of this book to cover the subject in detail. (Interested readers are forwarded to [13]). In this section, the choice of modem techniques is discussed, highlighting the various advantages and disadvantages of each method.

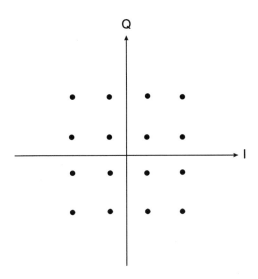

FIGURE 2.8 Constellation points in a 16-QAM system.

In selecting a modem, the following requirements should be met:

- High spectral efficiency, which maximizes capacity;
- High-power efficiency;
- Robust to multipath propagation effects;
- Low cost and ease of implementation;
- Low carrier-to-cochannel interference ratio;
- Low out-of-band radiation;
- Constant or near constant envelope.

In choosing a modulation scheme, power efficiency and spectrum efficiency are some of the issues that need to be addressed, so the system can be designed appropriately. Modulation techniques are often classified into two categories—constant envelope and nonconstant envelope. The former includes schemes such as GMSK, where only the phase is modulated, whereas the latter consists of schemes such as $\pi/4$-QPSK, QAM, QPSK, where both phase and amplitude are modulated. A power-efficient modem is often defined as one that can operate at a low E_b/N_o environment. Power efficiency in a modem is important to the design of a mobile communications terminal. Using a power-inefficient modem will have higher battery consumption and, in a portable terminal, power management, battery size, and charging intervals are important issues. A power-hungry modem will require larger battery packs, which will ultimately reduce its portability. If compromised with a smaller battery capacity, the terminal may have a shorter connection or talk time.

Although $\pi/4$-QPSK is more spectrally efficient, it is not very power efficient because it is a nonconstant envelope modulation scheme, requiring linear amplification. GMSK, on the other hand, is a constant envelope modulation scheme, which can be nonlinearly amplified without any major spectral spreading effects. Hence, it is more power efficient. It is, however, not as spectrally efficient as $\pi/4$-QPSK. For mobile portable terminals, Class C nonlinear power amplification is often preferred to save supplied DC power and improve the efficiency of the amplifier output stage.

2.6 CONCLUSION

The choice of a modulation scheme is important in the design of a mobile data communications system because it affects the performance of the system, the capacity (from the perspective of spectral efficiency), and the design of the terminals. In this chapter, several fundamental and advanced modulation schemes have been covered, and issues such as implementation and performance have been discussed. In order to accommodate for future high-capacity multiservice networks, new modulation schemes will be required to achieve the necessary performance and to utilize the already congested radio spectrum efficiently.

References

[1]   Stremler, F.G., *Introduction to Communication Systems*, 3rd Edition, Reading, MA: Addison Wesley, 1990.

[2]   Sklar, B., *Digital Communications*, Englewood Cliffs, NJ: Prentice Hall, 1988.

[3]   Yoshida, S., and F. Ikegami, "A Comparison of Multipath Distortion Characteristics among Digital Modulation Techniques," *IEEE Transactions on Vehicular Technology*, VT-34, New York, Aug. 1985, pp. 128–135.

[4]   Haykin, S., *Digital Communications*, New York: John Wiley and Sons, 1988.

[5]   Bohm B., J.A. Schoonees, and R.M. Braun, "Data to Frequency Mappings in Various MSK Schemes," *IEE Electronics & Communications Engineering Journal*, February 1994, pp. 13–20.

[6]   Pasupathy, S., "Minimum Shift Keying: A Spectrally Efficient Modulation," *IEEE Communications Magazine*, Vol. 17, Issue 4, July 1979, pp. 14–22.

[7]   Murota, K., and H. Hirade, "GMSK Modulation for Digital Mobile Radio Telephony," *IEEE Transactions on Communications*, COM-29, No. 7, New York, pp. 1,044–1,050.

[8]   Feher, K., "MODEMS for Emerging Digital Cellular-Mobile Radio System," *IEEE Transactions on Vehicular Technology*, Vol. VT-40, No. 2, St. Louis, MO, May 1991, pp. 355–365.

[9]   Goodman D.J., "Second-Generation Wireless Information Networks," *IEEE Transactions on Vehicular Technology*, Vol. VT-40, No. 2, St. Louis, MO, May 1991, pp. 366–374.

[10] Feher, K., ed., *Advanced Digital Communications*, Englewood Cliffs, NJ: Prentice Hall, 1987.

[11] Feher, K., Engineers of Hewlett Packard, *Telecommunications, Measurements, Analysis, & Instrumentation*, Englewood Cliffs, NJ: Prentice Hall, 1987.

[12] Webb, W.T., "QAM: The Modulation Scheme for Future Mobile Radio Communications?" *IEE Electronic and Communications Engineering Journal*, August 1992, pp. 167–176.

[13] Feher, K., *Digital Communications: Satellite and Earth Engineering*, Englewood Cliffs, NJ: Prentice Hall.

CHAPTER 3
▼▼▼

CHARACTERISTICS OF THE RADIO PROPAGATION CHANNEL

The radio channel is attractive due to its ability to provide wireless communications services, but it is also one of the most hostile mediums in which to operate. The propagation of electromagnetic waves are often reflected, scattered, diffracted, and attenuated by the surrounding environment. The scattered components interfere and build up an irregular field distribution, and the signal at the receiver is therefore attenuated and distorted.

In this chapter, the various transmission impairments in the radio channel are discussed, together with signal fading characteristics and the variation of the signal strengths in outdoor and indoor radio environments. The contributing mechanisms, such as delay and Doppler spreads, are also addressed. In mobile data communications, it is inadequate to look just at the signal variations alone. The bit-error-rate (BER) characteristics must also be analyzed for error mechanisms so that appropriate measures such as error control or diversity can be applied to ensure that data integrity is maintained. This chapter also looks at the factors that contribute to the error rates in the radio medium, and the error rates in the outdoor and indoor radio environments are also discussed. To take the effects of multipath propagation further, the performance of modulation schemes are briefly discussed in the mobile radio channel. In order that the reader may be able to appreciate the various transmission impairments, some radio propagation measurements have also been included, to illustrate and to provide a feel for the characteristics of the radio propagation channel.

3.1 CLASSIFICATION OF THE RADIO CHANNEL

In order to understand the radio propagation transmission impairments, it is important to characterize the channels. Channels are often classified into narrowband and wideband channels, which are often differentiated by the maximum delay spread, τ_{max} of the channel. The delay spread has the effect of stretching a signal in time such that the duration of a signal received is greater than that originally transmitted. This is due to multipath propagation and is detailed later in the chapter. The following relationship between the maximum delay spread and the bit period is often used to differentiate between narrowband and wideband channels.

$$\tau_{max} < T = \text{narrowband, normalized delay spread} < 1$$

$$\tau_{max} > T = \text{wideband, normalized spread} > 1$$

where

T = bit period
τ_{max} = the maximum delay spread of the channel.

A common way of representing delay spreads is by normalizing them to the bit period, τ/T, which can also be used to distinguish between narrowband and wideband systems. In narrowband systems, the path loss and fading statistics are often of interest. These include the rate of decay of signal strength with distance and the statistics of the fading encountered. In wideband systems, the delay spread characteristics are usually of primary concern, as they may cause intersymbol interference.

3.2 TRANSMISSION IMPAIRMENTS

In the mobile radio propagation channel, the following transmission impairments are experienced: multipath fading, path loss, and signal shadowing [1,2]. Multipath fading can be further categorized into frequency-selective fading and time-selective fading. Path loss is due to the relative rate of signal degradation with distance and is different in outdoor and indoor environments; hence, it will be dealt with separately. Signal shadowing occurs in all environments when the signal path is blocked due to buildings or furniture. These different transmission impairments will be dealt with in the following section.

3.2.1 Multipath Fading

Multipath fading is the phenomenon whereby the amplitude of the signals arriving at the receiver is the vector summation of randomly phased signal components caused by reflection, such as bouncing off walls/buildings, in the multipath medium. The summation of the signal amplitudes at the receiver usually tend towards a statistical distribution, more commonly known as Rayleigh or Rician distributions.

The complex representation of a signal propagating in the multipath radio channel is best represented by the impulse response of the radio channel [3]. The representation is a mathematical model illustrated as

$$h(t) = \sum_{m=1}^{L} A_m \delta(t - \tau_m) e^{j\varphi_m}$$

where the transmitted impulse $\delta(t)$ is received as the sum of L paths with amplitudes A_m and arrival times τ_m with phases φ_m.

Both A_m and φ_m are slowly varying random quantities, where A_m is a random varying quantity with a Rayleigh or Rician distribution and φ_m is a random variable with a uniform distribution from 0 to 2. This model is often adopted and used as a standard model [4,5].

The mobile or portable radio channel has a large number of unresolved paths, which results in a large number of random signals at each delay. As L becomes large, which is assumed in the model, h(t) tends by the Central Limit Theorem [6,7] to a complex Gaussian process (the Central Limit Theorem states that the probability distribution function of the sum of a large number of random variables approaches a Gaussian distribution). Hence, the fluctuations at each delay for the mobile radio channel can be approximated by Gaussian random processes. A_m is a random Rayleigh distributed variable because of φ_m, the phase component. This phase component is the cause of the signal cancellation effect. As each wave goes through the multipath environment, it is reflected and its phase is altered randomly. The detected signals, due to the mobile propagation environment, arrive at the receiver slightly delayed from each other with a random distribution of phase angles. Assuming a two-path propagation model, when signals from each path arrive at the receiver out of phase from the other path, the net result is a weaker signal. Taking the worst case, if they arrive 180° out of phase, the signals will completely cancel each other out if they are of equal amplitude. The opposite applies to in-phase signals, where they produce a net stronger signal. It is this superposition or summation of many randomly phased components that causes the signal amplitude to fluctuate. In the radio environment, the fluctuation of the signal amplitude tends to a Rayleigh distribution, and this is known as Rayleigh fading. The Rayleigh probability density function (PDF) [2] is shown in Figure 3.1. Conventional mobile radio channels have envelope statistics often represented by Rayleigh fading. However, in smaller high-capacity microcells, the fading statistics have tended to a Rician distribution [8–11]. In general, it has been found that when there is no direct path between the transmitter and receiver, the envelope tends to Rayleigh [4,12–14]. When there is direct line of sight between the transmitter and receiver, the fading tends towards a Rician distribution, which is illustrated in Figure 3.2.

The Rician distribution is often characterized by the K factor, which is defined as the ratio between the signal power in the dominant path to the signal power in the scattered paths. Rician distributed envelopes are often observed in the outdoor microcellular radio environment, and the fading of Rician envelopes is never as severe as that of Rayleigh distributed envelopes, due to the presence of the line of sight. The decrease in K factor means that the dominant path is diminishing, and a K factor of 0 indicates that the distribution has become Rayleigh.

3.2.2 Frequency-Selective Fading

The radio medium is a dispersive medium. Time dispersion is the result of the received signal having been propagated over many different paths of different lengths, suffering from different propagation delays. The spread of the signal can be observed from the impulse response of the radio channel. The time when the impulse signal is first detected at the receiver and the subsequent copies of it arriving at a delayed time is known as the spread of the signal, or more commonly known as the delay spread. The delay spread in a high bit-rate digital system (wideband) causes

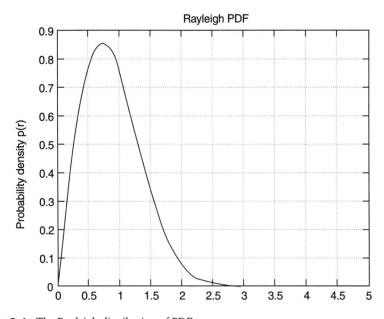

FIGURE 3.1 The Rayleigh distribution of PDF.

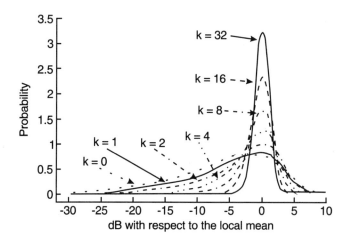

FIGURE 3.2 The Rician density function normalized to the local mean. (*Source:* [10].)

bit symbols to overlap and smear with the preceding and following symbols, giving rise to a phenomenon known as intersymbol interference (ISI).

To characterize the delay spread of a channel, the transfer function of the impulse response or the power-delay profile is used. The power-delay profile [14] involves the variation of the relative power density of the signal received to the delay of the path arrivals. Figure 3.3 is an example of a power-delay profile. It can be expressed as [15]:

$$P(\tau) = \sum_i A_i^2 \times \delta\,(\tau - \tau_i)$$

where

τ = delay spread
τ_i = delay of the ith path
A_i = amplitude of the ith path.

Narrowband channels are often said to exhibit frequency nonselective fading because the spectrum of the transmitted signal is narrow enough to ensure that all frequency components within the transmitted spectrum are affected in a similar way. This is often known as frequency-flat fading, and the signal is only impaired by multipath amplitude fading, as described in the previous section. However, in wideband channels, where the transmission bandwidth is large, as frequency components are further apart, the behavior at one frequency differs from that at another frequency because the electrical length of the signal is a function of frequency. To

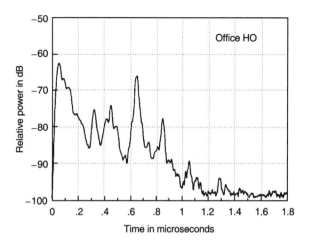

FIGURE 3.3 Power-delay profile. (*Source:* [14].)

define the frequency selectivity of a channel, the coherence bandwidth (CB) of the channel is examined in the following relationship.

$$CB = \frac{1}{2\pi\tau_{max}}$$

When the bandwidth of the transmitted signal is greater than the CB of the channel, frequency-selective fading is experienced, and when the transmitted bandwidth is less than the CB of the channel, frequency nonselective fading is the fading mechanism. Since the CB of the channel is a function of the maximum delay spread, τ_{max} of the channel, when the delay spread of the channel is high, there is a high probability that frequency-selective fading will occur.

3.2.3 Time-Selective Fading

Time-selective fading is primarily caused by the signal duration in the multipath channel. When the duration of a signal is greater than the coherence time (a measure of how rapidly the fading process can change) of the channel, the signal will undergo time-selective fading.

The coherence time (CT) of the channels possesses a relationship to the Doppler spread of the channel, similar to the relationship between the coherence bandwidth and the delay spread; i.e., CT is inversely proportional to the Doppler spread [16]. Hence, when the channel experiences large Doppler spreads as in the mobile radio propagation channel (not so much in the indoor channel), there is a likely chance that the signal propagating in the channel will undergo time-selective fading, as the CT of the channel decreases. Doppler spread is a measure of the spectral width of a received carrier when a sinusoidal carrier is transmitted over the multipath fading channel. It arises from the relative motion of the transmitter and receiver, causing a frequency shift. This frequency shift varies according to velocity, direction, and the scatterers involved in the path, and introduces random frequency modulation on the signal.

A portable terminal moving in a direction making an angle α with respect to the signal received from the i-th path has its carrier frequency f_c modified to [17]

$$f_c + f_d \cos\alpha$$

where

f_d = v/λ or $v f_c / c$
and v = speed of portable,
f_c = carrier frequency
and c = velocity of light.

The Doppler frequency can be positive or negative, depending on the angle of arrival α, producing a Doppler shift of $\pm f_d$ and, hence, random frequency modulation on the signal.

3.3 CLASSIFYING THE MULTIPATH FADING CHANNEL

In the multipath fading channel where various transmission impairments contribute to the distortion of the signal, it is important to understand the factors affecting the degradation of the signal. The coherence bandwidth and coherence time of the channel help us to classify the multipath fading channel. When the bandwidth of a transmission is higher than the coherence bandwidth of the channel, the time dispersion of the channel becomes significant and frequency-selective fading is said to occur. Similarly, when the duration of a signal is greater than the coherence time of the channel, frequency dispersion becomes significant and time-selective fading is present. This is summarized in Figure 3.4.

When a channel is both flat in time and frequency, it is then known as a flat-flat or a flat-fading channel. When the CB of the channel is exceeded but the signal duration is within the limits of the CT, the channel is then said to be time flat or time invariant but frequency selective. When the CT of the channel is exceeded and the bandwidth of transmission does not exceed CT, the channel is said to be frequency flat or frequency invariant, but time selective. Finally, when CT and CB are both exceeded, the channel is both frequency and time selective and is neither time or frequency flat. Such a channel is said to be nonflat.

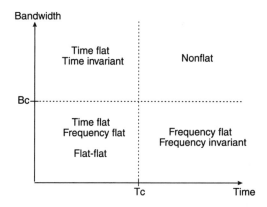

FIGURE 3.4   Multipath fading channel classification.

3.4 SHADOWING

Signal shadowing is experienced by both indoor and outdoor mobile radio communications. This impairment is primarily caused by attenuation in the form of signal-path blockage due to the surrounding environment. This is important in mobile radio but particularly important in buildings, because the propagation environment varies as people move around in the transmission paths. Also, in the indoor environment, furniture and partitions contribute to losses due to signal shadowing. Shadowing is also known as slow fading, and is found to follow a log-normal distribution for both indoors and outdoors [18].

3.5 PATH LOSS

Path loss is a quantitative measure of the amount of signal strength lost as the signal propagates from the transmitter to the receiver; i.e., path loss increases with distance. The path losses in the outdoor environment differ from that of indoor, due to the difference in the nature of the surroundings. As a result, they will be treated separately in the following sections.

3.5.1 Path Loss—Outdoor

Path losses often decay according to the path-loss exponent, which is inversely proportional to the distance. In free space the signal decays at a rate inversely proportional to the square of the distance between the transmitter and receiver. Hence, when a receiver is in the near field of the antenna, the signal will decay at a rate of d^{-2}. When the receiver moves further away from the antenna into the far field, the signal will decay at a faster rate, typically d^{-4}.

In the outdoor mobile radio propagation environment, the signal propagation is often modeled by a two-ray model, shown in figure 3.5. There is often a direct path between the transmitter and receiver and a ground reflected path. A commonly adopted model for urban microcells [8,9,10,11] is that when a line of sight (LOS) exists between the transmitter and receiver, the path-loss decay index is approximately free space, close to the transmitter. However, when the distance between the transmitter and receiver increases, the decay index increases to a fourth power law or more depending on the environment. It is often difficult to predict or estimate the path loss in urban environments, due to the strong dependence of signal propagation to environmental factors such as density and height of buildings, width of street, etc. Traditionally, field strength prediction models such as Okumura-Hata [19,20], Ibrahim-Parsons [21], Bloomquist-Ladell [22], and Longley-Rice [23] have been used to predict the path loss or signal-strength degradation for land mobile radio services [24,25], in urban and rural environments. These models, although widely used for conventional mobile radio, have not been found to be suitable for the field-strength prediction in microcells in high-density urban environments. This is due to the complex nature of the environment, and advanced techniques such as ray tracing [8,26,27] should be used instead.

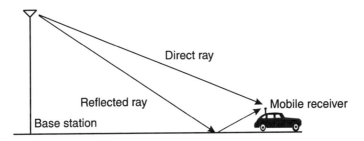

FIGURE 3.5 Two-ray mobile radio propagation model.

3.5.2 Path Loss—Indoor

In the indoor propagation environment, the radio signal strength decays much faster than that in the outdoor environment, and coverage is very much contained to a small area due the presence of walls, etc. Within buildings, walls, floors, and furniture serve to attenuate and scatter radio signals and the location, orientation, and electrical properties of these scatterers often affect the signal propagation. One of the most commonly adopted and comprehensive models is one that considers the signal propagation through various floors and walls with distance. This path loss model is described by the following equation [18,28]:

$$\text{Path loss} = \text{Unit Loss} + 10n \log (d) = kF + lW$$

- Unit loss is the power loss (dB) at 1m distance and typically specified as 30 dB;
- n is the power-decay index—n typically takes a value between 3.5 [28] and 4 but often depends on the propagation environment;
- d is the distance between the transmitter and receiver;
- k is the number of floors the signal traversed;
- F is the loss per floor;
- l is the number of walls the signal traversed;
- W is the loss per wall.

It has been widely adopted as an empirical model for indoor radio propagation due to its simplicity and ease of use, and it is used in various system-performance simulations in buildings [28].

3.6 SUMMARY OF PROPAGATION MEASUREMENTS IN VARIOUS ENVIRONMENTS

We have addressed several issues related to the mobile radio propagation environment and its transmission impairments. In this section, we outline some propagation measurements (wideband and narrowband) in various environments to provide the reader with an idea of typical propagation parameters. In order to differentiate between the various environments we will categorize the areas into outdoor, outdoor to indoor, and indoor environments.

3.6.1 Outdoor Measurements

Outdoor environments can be further categorized into urban, suburban, and rural areas. Wideband propagation measurements conducted in urban areas typically reveal an RMS delay spread in the region of 2 µseconds (µs), with a minimum of 1 µs and a maximum of 3µs, and this spread has been observed in various cities, including New York and Washington in the U.S. and London and Birmingham in the U.K. [29–32].

In suburban areas, the delay spreads are slightly less than those in urban areas, due to fewer scatterers present. In most measurements conducted, the RMS delay spread varied between 0.25 µs [33] and 2 µs [24,32,34]. In rural areas, the delay spreads have been found to vary up to as high as 12µs [24] in the U.K.

The GSM system in Europe has a bit period of 3.69 µs (for the data rate of 270 Kbps). In order for the GSM system to operate successfully without intersymbol interference caused by symbol overlap from delayed/echoed pulses, some form of adaptive equalization is required. The data structure in GSM incorporates a 26-bit Viterbi equalizer training sequence, which equips mobiles to tolerate up to 15 µs of delay spread, making them capable of operating in most environments.

Field strength measurements (using narrowband techniques) are often conducted to measure the signal-strength degradation between the transmitter and receiver. Regression (best-fit) lines are often plotted to model and estimate the path-loss characteristics. These models have been described briefly in the previous section.

3.6.2 Outdoor-to-Indoor Measurements

In mobile data communications, where data or computer terminals can equally be operating in outdoor or indoor environments, indoor signal coverage must also be considered. In order to ensure that radio signal coverage is available indoors, outdoor-to-indoor signal penetration loss must also be considered. Penetration or building loss is defined as the difference in the received signal inside a building and the average of the received signal around the perimeter of that building [35]. The loss is found to be dependent on the construction materials of a building, its orientation, its layout, its height, the percentage of windows, and the frequency. The variability of signal strength indoors makes prediction extremely difficult. However, in general it has been observed that the rate of decay or distance power law varies between 3.0 and 6.2, with an average of 4.5 [36]. Building attenuation (loss) tends to vary between 2 dB and 38 dB. The figure of 2 dB corresponds to modern buildings with predominantly glass outer structure. More detailed specific penetration losses have been characterized and can be found in [37–39].

3.6.3 Indoor Measurements

Within the last decade, there has been growing interest in radio propagation measurements indoors, for the provision of wireless communications services inside buildings. More recently, applications have not been limited to voice, but extend to data as well. Currently, data applications exists in the form of wireless electronic point-of-sale terminals, wireless modems, and higher bit-rate wireless local area networks (see Chapter 9).

Much work has been done in characterizing indoor radio propagation in buildings [40–45]. [36] summarizes and provides a good review of existing literature on indoor (including indoor penetration) propagation. In characterizing indoor radio propagation, much must be known about the environment, as signal strength depends very much on factors such as open plan offices, construction (brick, concrete, etc.), density of personnel, furniture, and other factors.

For narrowband measurements, it has been observed that path-loss exponents vary between 2 and 6 depending on the environment, the majority of which range between 2.5 and 4 [46]. Wall losses typically range between 10 dB and 15 dB, and floor losses range between 12 dB and 27 dB; however, this is again variable and dependent on the building construction. With reference to the ETSI indoor propagation model described earlier, these values are often used in the model to predict the radio signal coverage indoors.

Wideband measurements (RMS delay spread) are important as they affect the maximum data rate achievable without equalization or diversity. As previously mentioned, excessive delay spreads cause bit overlapping or smearing, which results in intersymbol interference. Most measurements conducted in indoor environments were found to vary between 15 ns and 100 ns in open plan office buildings. However, they can vary by up to 250 ns.

Figure 3.6 illustrates the variability of the signal strength measured in a typical indoor environment with 100 ns delay spread. The measurements were taken from a DECT test bed [47–49] (see Chapter 8) operating at 1.8 GHz indoors. Transmitted packet sizes of 364 bits were measured for their mean signal strength over a duration of approximately 35 seconds (each packet was transmitted in a time slot, the period of which was 10 ms), with a receiver moving at a speed of 0.5 meters per second (m/s). It was observed that the signal varied very widely and took dips of fades 20 dB or more. The fades were due to several contributing factors or error mechanisms causing error bursts. They will be studied in the following section.

3.7 ERROR MECHANISMS

It is crucial for the provision of a data service in the mobile radio channel to understand the causes of errors so that appropriate measures can be taken to ensure that a reasonable link quality can be maintained. In the mobile radio channel, errors tend to occur in bursts due to the error mechanisms present. An error burst is often characterized by a region of consecutive errors followed by a stream of consecutive error-free bits. It is often defined as the number of bits between two successive erroneous bits, including the two bits in error. The region of errored bits must be followed by a region of error-free bits whose length must be equal to or longer than the run length of the region of errors.

In most applications, the error bursts often impose a limit on the intelligibility of the information transmitted. Very often, a 10^{-3} BER limit is used—on average 1 bit error in every 1,000 bits. This limit is typically used for voice applications. However, a more stringent limit is imposed for data, typically 10^{-6}, which is sometimes difficult to achieve. In order to understand the error rates in the radio channel and how to overcome this disadvantage, we shall look at the error mechanism in greater detail.

As previously mentioned, the radio channel suffers from periodic fades as the mobile moves in the radio environment. When the signal level is in a fade—i.e., it drops below the signal threshold—bursts of errors are likely to occur and the time that it falls below this limit provides an estimate of the size of the error burst. The average duration of a fade (ADF) is often characterized by the following equation [2].

$$\text{ADF} = \frac{\sqrt{2\pi}\left[e^{R^2} - 1\right]}{\beta v R}$$

where β is a frequency dependent variable and is equal to $2\pi/\lambda$, v is the speed of the mobile in m/s, and R is the fade depth expressed as a ratio of the RMS signal level.

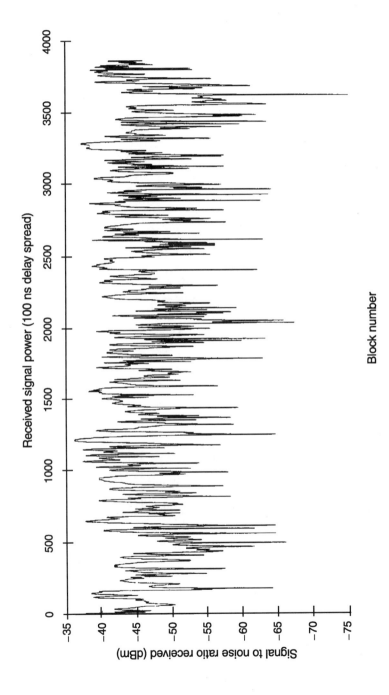

FIGURE 3.6   Signal level variability for indoor portable terminals.

The average fade duration of a signal depends on the propagation frequency and speed of the mobile.

In the outdoor environment, a mobile operating at 900 MHz and traveling at 50 km/hr undergoes an average fade depth of 20 dB. The average fade duration for this case is 0.962 ms. However, when compared to a slow moving portable terminal operating at the same frequency and average fade depth at a walking speed of 0.5 m/s, the average fade duration is 26.7 ms. Hence, the portable suffers considerably larger error bursts due to the longer time it spends in a fade than does a mobile. The case for the portable terminal also applies to portable terminals in indoor environments, such as cordless systems like CT2 or DECT, which will be described in Chapter 8. Figures 3.7 and 3.8 illustrates a typical mobile radio signal at 900 MHz undergoing signal amplitude fluctuation. The figures show in time, the envelope of the mobile, and portable terminals traveling at 50 km/hr and 1.8 km/hr, respectively, through a Rayleigh fading environment. Note the fade duration and depth that the mobile and portable terminals undergo. It can be observed that the signal variation is much faster for the mobile than for the portable, which means that the average time spent in a fade for the mobile is shorter than for the portable. Hence, the portable is more likely to suffer larger error bursts.

It was observed in [50–52] that burst errors occur in regions where the signal-to-noise ratio falls below a threshold level, and very often the error burst lengths are

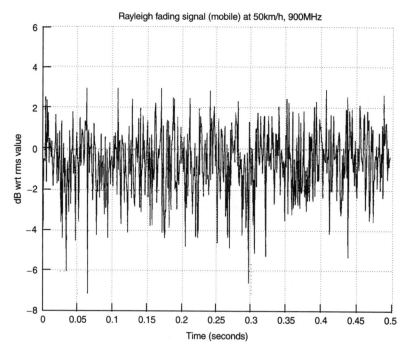

FIGURE 3.7 Mobile radio signal fluctuation at 50 km/hr.

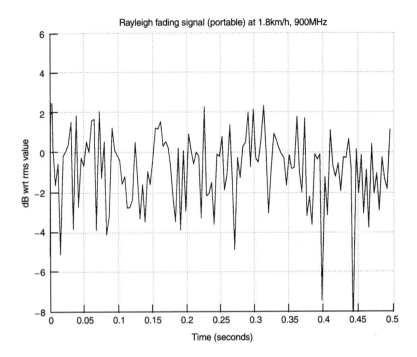

FIGURE 3.8 Portable radio signal fluctuation at 1.8 km/hr.

large. These conditions render forward error correction (FEC) coding useless and will require error control in the form of automatic repeat request (ARQ) instead. FEC techniques are useful for a range of BER, and large bursts of errors will not be correctable. As a result, using FEC will be ineffective, serving only to impose additional overheads. Considerations to error-control techniques are treated in more detail in the following chapter.

Very often, at low signal-to-noise ratio levels, additional mechanisms contribute to the causes of burst errors, such as loss of synchronization. In the outdoor mobile environment, the signal undergoes Doppler spreads, which introduces random frequency modulation on the signal and may cause carrier recovery problems at the receiver. In addition, it has also been observed that error bursts were often found to increase in frequency as the normalized delay spread (τ/T) increases. The error bursts also tend to occur irrespective of the Doppler frequency, indicating that delay spread plays a larger role in its contribution to error mechanisms [53–55]. At large delay spreads, when τ/T is greater than 0.5, delay spread is the major dominant error mechanism caused by imperfect sample timing, resulting in error bursts. It has also been observed that at low delay spreads, when $\tau/T < 0.2$, envelope fading is the major contributing factor, and when $\tau/T > 0.2$, timing/clock recovery and delay spread are the main error mechanisms [3,56].

The error bursts in the radio channel have the effect of corrupting information, and, in the area of data applications, techniques to enhance the performance of the radio channel must be incorporated to overcome the error mechanisms present. One of the most efficient and widely used techniques is the use of antenna diversity [4,57], which can provide approximately a 10 dB improvement in performance. (Antenna diversity is the technique whereby two antennas, separated by a distance of $\lambda/2$, receive signals that are uncorrelated. The receiver instantaneously selects the antenna with the higher signal strength or the lower error rate.) [12,58,59]. This technique requires additional hardware at the receiver, which increases cost.

Error-control and channel-coding techniques such as FEC and ARQ are also useful to increase the performance of a radio link. FEC techniques improve the quality of a link by lowering the fade margin with the coding gain achieved through a coding scheme (coding gain is the difference in values of signal energy per bit-to-noise ratio required to attain a particular error rate with and without coding). However, there is a limitation to FEC in that it is optimum only for a range of bit error rate and type of errors—it can correct up to a certain error pattern or burst and may not be applicable to portable or slowly varying radio channels where large bursts occur. Chapter 4 addresses this issue in greater detail.

3.8 EVALUATING THE LINK PERFORMANCE

The quality of a link is often evaluated using an eye pattern [60], which provides a qualitative first approximation of the system performance. Eye patterns are also often used to study the performance of a modulation scheme such as in a mobile radio channel. An eye pattern can be generated on an oscilloscope by feeding the bit rate clock to the external trigger of the scope and feeding the signal to the y input. With the horizontal time base set approximately to the symbol duration, an eye pattern can be achieved. The eye reveals several features that indicate the performance of a digital communications system. In the eye pattern shown in Figure 2.9, two important indicators are the width and height of the eye. The width of the eye indicates the time interval over which the received signal can be optimally sampled free of errors due to ISI. The preferred time of sampling is the instant at which the eye is open widest. ISI is often caused by multipath propagation effects in the radio medium, where multiple copies of a signal arrives at the receiver at different delayed intervals. The phenomena is explained in the previous sections. Another characteristic of the eye pattern is the height of the eye, which defines the margin over noise or the radio S/N degradation. When the eye closes (the height of the eye decreases), the signal may be in a fade and burst errors are likely to occur. The eye width also has something to tell about the expected performance of a modulation scheme. When the eye width is narrowed, any slight offset of sampling timing will result in severe S/N degradation, increasing the probability of an error burst.

The performance of modulation schemes in a typical mobile radio channel using eye diagram techniques have been studied in [61]. It was observed that BPSK is the most resistant to mobile radio transmission impairments such as frequency-selective fading. BPSK is robust against delay spreads as long as the normalized delay spread τ/T is less than 1. For other modulation schemes other than BPSK, such as QPSK and MSK, the eye height diminishes with increasing τ/T and the width of the eye is narrowed at the same time.

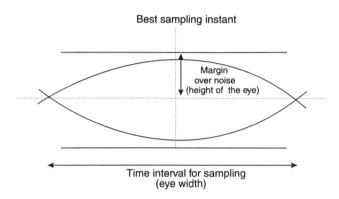

Best sampling instant

Margin over noise (height of the eye)

Time interval for sampling (eye width)

FIGURE 3.9 An eye diagram.

3.9 CONCLUSIONS

The various transmission impairments and their effect on the quality of the radio channel have been addressed. Typically, delay spreads, Doppler spreads, and multipath fading are the main issues concerning the condition of the radio channel. However, when analyzed in detail, all of these factors add up in some way to cause error bursts. A brief summary of propagation measurements in various environments has also been included solely for the reader to have a feel for the respective environments. The values indicated should not to be taken as typical due to the strong dependency of measurements on the surroundings. The chapter addressed the error characteristics in various radio environments and briefly considered the techniques that can be used to enhance the performance of the radio signal in error-prone channels. Detailed references to the appropriate topics have also been included for further study.

References

[1]   Lee, W.C.Y., *Mobile Communications Engineering*, New York: McGraw-Hill, 1982.
[2]   Lee, W.C.Y., *Mobile Communications Design Fundamentals*, Howard W SAMS, Indiana, 1986.
[3]   Chuang, J.C.I., "The Effects of Time Delay Spread on Portable Radio Communications," IEEE J-SAC-5, June 1987, pp. 879–889.

[4]   Jakes, W.C., "Microwave Mobile Communications," New York: John Wiley and Sons, 1974.

[5]   Bello, P.A., "Characterisation of Randomly Time Variant Linear Channels," IEEE Transactions on Communication Systems CS-11, Dec. 1963, pp. 360–393.

[6]   Peebles, P.Z., Jr., "Probability, Random Variables, and Random Signal Principles," New York: McGraw-Hill, 1987.

[7]   Cox, D.C., "Universal Digital Portable Radio Communications," *IEEE Proceedings*, Vol. 75, No. 4, April 1987, pp. 436–477.

[8]   Chia, S.T.S., R. Steele, E. Green, and A. Baran, "Propagation and Bit Error Ratio Measurements for a Microcellular System," Journal of the IERE, Vol. 57, No. 6, (supplement), Nov/Dec. 1987, pp. S255–266.

[9]   Green, E., "Path Loss and Signal Variability Analysis for Microcells," *Proc. Fifth IEE International Conference on Mobile Radio and Personal Communications*, Warwick, U.K., Dec. 1989, pp. 38–42.

[10] Green, E., "Radio Link Design for Microcellular Systems," British Telecom Technology Journal, Vol. 8, No. 1, January 1990, pp. 85–96.

[11] Green, E., and M. Hata, "Microcellular Propagation Measurements in an Urban Environment," *Proc. IEEE International Conference on Personal, Indoor, and Mobile Radio Communications*, PIMRC, London, U.K., 1991, pp. 324–328.

[12] Wilkinson, T.A., "Channel Modelling and Link Simulation Studies for the DECT Test Bed Program," *Proc. 6th IEE International Conference on Mobile Radio and Personal Communications*, IEE Conference Record 351, Warwick, U.K., Dec. 1991, pp. 293–299.

[13] Wilkinson, T.A., "Link Simulation Studies for the DECT Test Bed," EC-COST 231TD(91)49, Stockholm.

[14] Devasirvatham, D.M.J., "Multipath Time Delay Spread in the Portable Radio Environment," *IEEE Communications Magazine*, Vol. 25, No 6e, June 1987, pp. 13–21.

[15] Prasad, R., B.J. Bout, and W.A. Schouten, "An Overview of Indoor Wireless Communications in the 20–60-GHz Region," EC-COST 231TD(92)1, Helsinki.

[16] Steele, R., *Mobile Radio Communications*, London: Pentech Press, 1992.

[17] Parsons, D.J., *The Mobile Radio Propagation Channel*, London: Pentech Press, 1992.

[18] Keenan, J.M., and A.J. Motley, "Radio Coverage in Buildings," *British Telecom Technology Journal*, Vol. 8 No. 1, Jan. 1990, pp. 19–24.

[19] Hata, M., "Empirical Formulae for Propagation Loss in Land Mobile Radio Services," *IEEE Transactions on Vehicular Technology*, Vol. VT-29, pp. 317–325.

[20] Okumura et al., "Field Strength and Its Variability in VHF and UHF Land Mobile Radio Service," *Review of the ECL*, Vol. 16, pp. 825–873.

[21] Ibrahim, M.F., and J.D. Parsons, "Signal Strength Prediction in Built-Up Areas, Part 1: Median Signal Strength," *Proc. IEE* Part F, Vol. 130, London, pp. 377–391.

[22] Bloomquist, A., and L. Ladell, "Prediction and Calculation of Transmission Loss in Different Types of Terrain," *AGARD Conference Publication*, Vol. CP-144, 32/1-25, 1974.

[23] Longley, A.G., and P.L. Rice, "Prediction of Tropospheric Radio Transmission Loss Over Irregular Terrain—A Computer Method," *ESSA Technical Report*, ERL79-ITS67, 1968.

[24] EC-COST 207, Final Report, "Digital Land Mobile Radio Communications," Commission of the European Communities, EUR 12160 EN, Brussels, 1989.

[25] COST 231 Subgroup Propagation Models, "Urban Transmission Loss Models for Mobile Radio in the 900 and 1800 MHz Bands," Revision 1, COST 231TD(90)119 Rev. 1, Florence, January 24, 1991.

[26] Wagen, J.F., "SIP Simulation of UHF Propagation in Urban Microcells," *Proc. IEEE Vehicular Technology Conference*, St. Louis, MO, May 1991, pp. 301–306.

[27] Berg, J.E., R. Bownds, and F. Lotse, "Path Loss and Fading Models for Microcells at 900 MHz," *Proc. IEEE Vehicular Technology Conference*, Denver, CO, May 1992 pp. 666–671.

[28] ETSI, "A Guide to DECT Features that Influence the Traffic Capacity and the Maintenance of a High Radio Link Quality, including the Results of Simulations," ETR, RES-03R(92)07, Valbonne, France.

[29] Cox, D.C., "910 MHz Urban Mobile Radio Propagation: Multipath Characteristics in New York City," *IEEE Transactions on Communications*, Vol. COM-21, No. 11, Nov. 1973, pp. 1,188–1,194.

[30] Cox, D.C., and R.P. Leck, "Distributions of Multipath Delay Spread and Average Excess Delay for 910 MHz Urban Mobile Radio Paths," *IEEE Transactions on Antennas and Propagation*, Vol. AP-23, No. 2, March 1975, pp. 206–213.

[31] Rappaport, T.S., S.Y. Seidel, and R. Singh, "900 MHz Multipath Propagation Measurements for US Digital Cellular Radiotelephone," *IEEE Transactions on Vehicular Technology*, Vol. 39, No 2, May 1990, pp. 132–139.

[32] Bajwa, A.S., "UHF Wideband Statistical Model and Simulation Of Multipath Propagation Effects," *IEE Proceedings F*, Vol. 132, Pt F, No. 5, London, August 1985, pp. 327–333.

[33] Cox, D.C., "Delay-Doppler Characteristics of Multipath Propagation at 910 MHz in a Suburban Mobile Radio Environment," *IEEE Transactions on Antennas and Propagation*, Vol. AP-20, No. 5, Sept. 1972, pp. 625–635.

[34] Van Rees, J., "Measurements of the Wideband Radio Channel Characteristics for Rural, Residential and Suburban Areas," *IEEE Transactions on Vehicular Technology*, Vol. VT-36, No. 1, February 1987, pp. 2–6.

[35] Rice, L.P., "Radio Transmission into Buildings at 35 and 150 MHz," *BSTJ*, Vol. 38, No. 1, pp. 197–210.

[36] Molkdar, D., "Review of Radio Propagation Into and Within Buildings," *IEE Proceedings H*, Vol. 138, No. 1, London, February 1991, pp. 61–73.

[37] Turkmani, A.M.D., J.D. Parsons, and D.G. Lewis, "Radio Propagation into Buildings at 441, 900, 1400 MHz," *Proc. 4th IEE International Conference on Land Mobile Radio*, Univ. of Warwick, Dec. 15–17, 1987, IEE Publication 78, pp. 129–139.

[38] Turkmani, A.M.D., and J.D. Parsons, "Measurement of Building Penetration Liss on Radio Signals at 441, 900, 1400 MHz," *Journal of the IERE*, Vol. 58, (6) Supplement, 1988, pp. 164–174.

[39] Wilkinson, T.A., and S.K. Barton, "Propagation in Buildings for Radio LANs," COST 231 TD(92)111, Helsinki, Sept. 8–11, 1992.

[40] Alexander, S.E. and G. Pugliese, "Cordless Communications within Buildings, Results of Measurements at 900 MHz and 60 GHz," *BTTJ*, Vol. 1, No. 1, July 1983, pp. 99–105.

[41] Alexander, S.E., "Characterising Buildings for Propagation at 900 MHz," *IEE Electronics Letters*, Vol. 19, No. 20, September 29, 1983, pp. 860.

[42] Devasirvatham, D.M.J., "Time Delay Spread Measurements of Wideband Radio Signals Within a Building," *IEE Electronics Letters*, Vol. 20, No. 23, 1984, pp. 950–951.

[43] Devasirvatham, D.M.J., "Time Delay Spread and Signal Level Measurements of 850 MHz Radio Waves in Building Environments," *IEEE Transactions on Antennas and Propagation*, Vol. AP-34, No. 11, Nov. 1986, pp. 1,300–1,305.

[44] Devasirvatham, D.M.J,. "Time Delay Spread Measurements at 850 MHz and 1.7 GHz inside a Metropolitan Office Building," *IEE Electronics Letters*, Feb. 2 1989, Vol. 25, No. 3, pp. 194–196.

[45] Devasirvatham, D.M.J., M.J. Krain, and D.A. Rappaport, "Radio Propagation Measurements at 850 MHz, 1.7 GHz, and 4 GHz inside Two Dissimilar Office Buildings," *IEE Electronics Letters*, Vol. 26, No. 7, March 29, 1990, pp. 445–447.

[46] Wilkinson, T.A., "Radio Propagation Channel Modelling for the DECT Test Bed," COST 231 TD(91)48, Sweden, June 4–7, 1991.

[47] Schultes, G., W. Simbürger, H. Novak, and M. Happl, "Physical and Medium Access Layer DECT Test Bed," COST 231TD(92)28, Leeds, England.

[48] Schultes et al., "A Testbed for DECT Physical and Medium Access Layers," *Proc. 3rd IEEE PIMRC*, Boston, October 19–21, 1992, pp. 349–355.

[49] Schultes, G, H. Knapp, W. Simbürger, and M. Happl, "Measurements of the Error Performance of a DECT Link in a Controlled Time Dispersive Environment," COST 231TD(92)41, Leeds, England.

[50] Omori, H., and K. Otani, "Burst Error Characteristics of Digital Land Mobile Radio," *IEEE Conference Record CH1506-5/80*, May 1980, pp. 24.2.1–5.

[51] Otani, K., and K. Daikoku, "Burst Error Performance Encountered in Digital Land Mobile Radio," *IEEE Transactions on Vehicular Technology*, VT-30, No. 4, Nov. 1981.

[52] Otani, K., and H. Omori, "Distribution of Burst Error Lengths in Rayleigh Fading Radio Channels," *IEE Electronics Letters*, 1990, Vol. 16, No. 23.

[53] Yoshida, S., F. Ikegami, and T. Takeuchi, "A Mechanism of Burst Error Occurrence Due to Multipath Propagation in Digital Mobile Radio," *Proc. International Symposium on Antennas and Propagation*, ISAP '85, Kyoto, Japan, Aug. 1985, pp. 561–564.

[54] Yoshida, S., S. Onoe, and F. Ikegami, "The Effect of Sample Timing on Bit-Error-Rate Performance in a Multipath Fading Channel," *IEEE Transactions on Vehicular Technology*, VT-35, Nov. 1986, pp. 168–174.

[55] Yoshida, S., F. Ikegami, and T. Takeuchi, "Causes of Burst Errors in Multipath Fading Channels," *IEEE Transactions on Communications*, Vol. 36, No. 1, January 1988, pp. 107–113.

[56] Chuang, J.C.I., "Modelling and Analysis of Digital Portable Communications Channels with Time Delay Spread," *Proc. of the IEEE International Conference on Communications*, June 1986, pp. 246–251.

[57] Acampora, A.S., and J.H. Winters, "System Applications for Wireless Indoor Communications," *IEEE Communications Magazine*, Vol. 25 No. 8, August 1987, pp. 11–19.

[58] Lopes, L.B., "On the Radio Link Performance of the DECT System," *Proc. of the IEEE Globecom '90 Conference*, IEEE CH2827-4/90/0000-1013, pp. 604.3.1–5.

[59] Lopes, L.B., "Performance of the DECT System in Fading Dispersive Channels," *IEE Electronics Letters*, Vol. 26, No. 17, Aug. 16, 1990, pp. 1416–1417.

[60] Feher, K., Engineers of Hewlett Packard, *Telecommunications, Measurements, Analysis, & Instrumentation*, Englewood Cliffs, NJ: Prentice Hall, 1987.

[61] Yoshida S., and F. Ikegami, "A Comparison of Multipath Distortion Characteristics Among Digital Modulation Techniques," *IEEE Transactions on Vehicular Technology*, VT-34, Aug. 1985, pp. 128–135.

CHAPTER 4
▼▼▼

ERROR-CONTROL TECHNIQUES FOR THE RADIO CHANNEL

In mobile radio communications in which the signal undergoes transmission impairments, such as intersymbol interference or multipath fading, the issue of error control is almost unavoidable, especially when concerned with the transmission of data. The subject of error control is a mature one and exists in various forms, which can be placed into 2 categories: forward error correction (FEC) [1–7] and automatic repeat request (ARQ) [8–11]. The main difference between the two schemes is that FEC does not need a feedback or return channel to carry out error correction, while ARQ requires a return channel to relay crucial retransmission information. FEC techniques are primarily used to detect and correct errors encountered in a radio channel, whereas ARQ schemes incorporate some form of error-detection code and corrects errors by requesting the retransmission of the errored blocks.

Error detection is the process whereby a code is used to detect for errors, and error correction involves using the code to correct errors. Error-correction codes often require error detection to locate the errors before they are corrected. Error-detection codes are only used to detect the location of errors.

The primary advantage of FEC is that it does not require a feedback channel and, hence, can operate in simplex mode. However, it has the drawback of overheads introduced by codes, which may lower the effective data throughput. ARQ does not impose large overheads, but it requires a feedback channel and must be able to tolerate propagation delays in both the forward and reverse directions. This chapter aims to cover the principles of such techniques, which are crucial to the reliability of information transmission over a radio link.

4.1 FORWARD ERROR CORRECTION

In designing a digital communications system, emphasis must be given to the reliable transmission of information—especially in the application of data, where integrity is crucial. With every transmission/modulation technique, there is an associated error probability, which is dependent on the transmitted signal energy per bit (E_b) and the noise encountered (N_o) [12]. Increasing the signal energy to noise ratio per bit (E_b/N_o) reduces the probability of error in transmission, however, practical considerations place a limit on the E_b/N_o. For a fixed E_b/N_o, the only way to lower the probability of error is to use coding. The use of coding techniques introduces coding gain, which is defined as the reduction in required signal power for a given error probability when coding is in use, compared with the signal power required for the same error probability without coding. The reduction in the required signal power is often exploited to reduce transmission power at the expense of reduced throughput, due to coding overheads.

FEC techniques can be split into two categories—block codes and convolutional codes—and they will be treated independently in the following sections. However, we will use the principle of block codes to illustrate an FEC system.

In a binary (n,k) block code, a sequence of k information or user data bits are algebraically related to n-k parity bits to give an overall encoded block of n bits. The efficiency of such a code is measured by its code rate, given by k/n. A typical FEC system, illustrated in Figure 4.1, is made up of an encoder, a transmitter/modulator, a channel, a receiver/demodulator, and a decoder. The input data stream is first encoded by adding redundant bits of information before the transmitter. At the transmitter, the encoded data stream is modulated appropriately and sent over the channel. The channel suffers from transmission impairments due to limitations of the medium, such as noise or fading. At the receiver, the data stream is then detected and demodulated, after which the received data stream is decoded back into its original form.

4.2 BLOCK CODES

The construction of a block code is shown in Figure 4.2a. The binary data source generates a sequence of symbols[1] at a rate of R symbols per second, which are then grouped into blocks of k symbols long. Each of these blocks are then encoded by

---

1. The word *symbols* is used in the general definition of block codes and should not be confused with bits. In some codes, each symbol is represented by one bit. However, multilevel or m-ary codes have each symbol represented by several bits. Reed Solomon codes, described in the following sections, are an example of this.

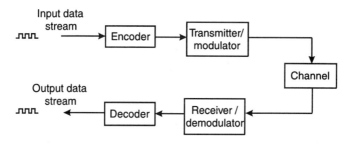

FIGURE 4.1 A forward error correction system.

appending (n-k) redundant parity symbols. The result of this is a (n,k) codeword, shown in Figure 4.2b, with k information symbols and n-k parity symbols, where n is the total number of symbols. At the receiver, decoding is achieved by determining the most likely transmitted codeword, given the received sequence Z, and the redundant symbols are then stripped away, leaving the information symbols.

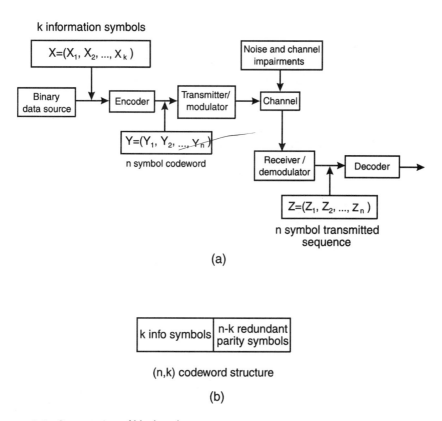

FIGURE 4.2 Construction of block codes.

4.2.1 Correction Power of Block Codes

In order to summarize the power of block codes, we first look at some definitions. The Hamming weight (w) of a codeword is defined as its number of nonzero components; i.e., if c = 10011, w(c) = 3. The Hamming distance (d) between two codewords is the number of positions in which they differ; i.e., if c_1 = 10011 and c_2 = 11000, then d (c_1,c_2) = 3. The distance between any two codewords is the Hamming weight of the sum of the codewords, and the minimum distance d_{min} of a linear block code is equal to the minimum weight of its nonzero codewords.

A block code possesses the following characteristics:

Detection of up to *s* errors per codeword	$d_{min} >= S + 1$
Correct up to *t* errors per codeword	$d_{min} >= 2t + 1$
Correct up to *t* errors and detect *s* > *t* errors simultaneously per codeword	$d_{min} >= S + t + 1$

4.2.2 Some Important Block Codes

For a (n,k) block code, the minimum distance is given by $d_{min} <= n - k + 1$ [7]. Examples of block codes include Bose-Chaudhuri-Hocquenghem (BCH); Reed-Solomon (RS); and Reed-Muller, Golay [13–16]. The following sections will present a summary of the power of some of the codes and their applications.

4.3 BOSE-CHAUDHURI-HOCQUENGHEM

The BCH code is one of the most important classes of linear block codes. A BCH code is a *t*-error-correcting code and is able to correct up to *t* random errors per codeword. The codes possess the following parameters. For any positive integer *m* (equal to or greater than 3) and *t* (less than $[2^m - 1]/2$), there exists a binary BCH code with

Block length	$n = 2^m - 1$
Number of message bits	$k >= n - mt$
Minimum distance	$d_{min} >= 2t + 1$

Further details of the BCH code can be found in [1,4,17].

BCH codes have found applications in various wireless communications systems. One of its more popular applications is in the paging system. The Post Office Code Standardization Advisory Group (POCSAG) code was developed in the U.K. as a paging standard through the joint efforts of Philips Research Laboratories and the British Post Office [18–20]. Designed for constant bit-rate transmission of 512 bps, the code format is based on 32-bit codewords comprising a (31,21) BCH code with a single even parity bit. The code has a Hamming distance of six and is able to correct five burst errors and two random errors. POCSAG has been widely adopted in many paging systems worldwide.

Another application of BCH codes is found in the cellular radio systems, where it has been used as part of the cellular data link control (CDLC) for data transmission over the cellular system [21]. This was originally developed by Racal in the U.K., based on the popular high-level data-link control (HDLC) standard as used in X.25 wide-area networks. The CDLC modem is based on the BCH (8,16) code and is a framed, bit-oriented, synchronous, full duplex data link protocol. To enable reliable data communications over the mobile radio channel, bit interleaving (a burst error-correction technique, which will be described in the following sections) and selective retransmission ARQ is incorporated together with the FEC. In addition, the BCH code has also been proposed for protecting facsimile signal transmission in digital mobile radio systems [22]. The version of the code proposed for facsimile transmission is the BCH (21,31) for a 4.8-Kbps user data stream. Bit interleaving is also employed to distribute the burst errors encountered in the radio channel. The BER performance of the code in the mobile radio channel at a signal-to-noise ratio of 14 dB was found to have a median of 10^{-4}. The laboratory-simulated fax transmission achieved a mean opinion-score rating of 3 (on a scale of 1 to 5, hence the transmission achieved only fair quality).

4.4 REED-SOLOMON CODES

Of great importance to mobile communications due to its error correction capability, Reed-Solomon code has been implemented in a variety of forms. RS codes are a subclass of nonbinary BCH codes and have been adopted as a popular FEC code for many data applications for radio communications.

RS codes operate on multibit symbols rather than individual bits. Hence, the RS encoder differs from a conventional binary encoder (such as the binary BCH encoder) because it is a multilevel code. The RS encoder for the (n,k) code on m-bit symbols groups the incoming data stream into blocks of *km* bits long. Each of these data blocks are then treated as *k* symbols, with each symbol having *m* bits. The encoder then expands these blocks of *k* symbols into *n* symbols by appending *n-k* redundant symbols for error detection and correction. The RS codes operating on *m* bit symbols possesses the following parameters:

Symbols	*m* bits per symbol
Block length	$n = 2^m - 1$ symbols or $m(2^m - 1)$ bits
Number of parity symbols	$n - k = 2t$ symbols or $m \times 2t$ bits
Minimum distance	$d_{min} = 2t + 1$ symbols

RS codes operating on 8-bit symbols are very popular and powerful [7]. Because it is a multilevel code, it is well suited for the correction of burst errors, as found in the fading mobile radio channel. The following example illustrates.

Example:

A single error correcting (t = 1) RS code operating on 2 bit symbols (*m* = 2) has four possible symbols (0, 1, 2, 3) and can be represented in binary as

0 = 00;
1 = 01;
2 = 10;
3 = 11.

This code possesses the following parameters:

$$n = 2^2 - 1 = 3 \text{ symbols} = 6 \text{ bits and}$$

$$n - k = 2t = 2 \text{ symbols} = 4 \text{ bits}$$

The code can therefore correct $(n - k)/2$ symbols, i.e., 1 symbol or 2 bits. Hence, if the codeword (0, 1, 2) is transmitted, i.e., (00 01 10), the decoder will be able to correct any inphase burst error of a length of 2 bits (spanning a symbol). Therefore, in general, a t symbol error-correcting RS code has the power to correct t inphase error bursts of length m bits in a codeword.

RS has been applied to data transmission over cellular radio. The CDLC modem described in previous section has an operational mode with RS encoding, based on the RS(72,68) codeword, for channels with fewer errors, which allows a higher user data rate. This is further detailed in Chapter 6. One of the more recent additions to RS FEC applications in the radio communications field is in the second-generation digital cordless systems. More commonly known as CT2, this cordless telepoint system originally developed in the U.K. [23] for a *cordless public telephone* service [24–26]. The system has also been adopted in Canada with a slightly different specification under the name of CT2Plus [27]. The European CT2 Standard ETS 300 131 defined by ETSI [28], specifies that RS coding be used for data transmission applications over the radio channel. The (63,k) RS code with 8 bit symbols is to be used for synchronous data transmission (where k varies between 2 and 40 for data transmission rates between 300 bps and 19,200 bps, respectively) and the (63,44) RS code to be used with ARQ (described in the following sections) for asynchronous data services. The difference between the Canadian and the European specifications for data is the number of bits per symbol used in the coding; the former uses 6-bit and the latter uses 8-bit symbols. The performances of the various schemes for asynchronous data transmission have been studied by [27]. For synchronous data applications, the various coding rates specified have been investigated [29] and, in general, it was found that ARQ will be required to achieve data reliability. This is due to the highly bursty nature of the slowly varying radio channel in which CT2 operates. This phenomena was observed in the previous chapter, with the long average duration of fades. As such, it will be difficult to implement a synchronous data service while maintaining data integrity through ARQ techniques. The performance of the CT2 system with RS coding at various rates will be discussed in further detail in Chapter 8, along with performance of ARQ protocols over the DECT system.

4.5 DECODING OF BLOCK CODES

The decoding of block codes can be done using various techniques. The most popular is the Berlekamp-Massey Algorithm (BMA) for RS and BCH codes [30–32]. Essentially, this algorithm is iterative and determines and calculates an error-locator polynomial, for solving its roots. This locates and defines the positions and magnitude of the errors. The detailed process is beyond the scope of this book, however, references [1–3,5,13] cover this technique very well, and some implementation of RS decoding algorithms is discussed in [33].

4.6 CONVOLUTIONAL CODES

Unlike block codes, where codewords are produced on a block-by-block basis, convolutional codes operate on the information data stream without splitting it up into blocks. Figure 4.3 shows a simple convolutional encoder. The general elements behind a convolutional encoder is the k stage shift register, v mod-2 (for binary convolutional codes) adders, a commutator, and a set of connections between k stages of the shift register and the v mod-2 adders. Information symbols are shifted in one at a time and the outputs from the mod-2 adders, determined by the connections to the shift register, are sampled in turn by the commutator to produce v output symbols. Since v output symbols are produced for each input symbol, the code rate is $1/v$. The rate of the code depends on the number of encoded symbols output. Higher rate codes can therefore be generated by shifting in more symbols. The constraint length of the encoder is equal to the length of the shift register, k.

4.7 DECODING OF CONVOLUTIONAL CODES

Convolutional codes are often decoded using Viterbi or sequential decoding [7,14,16,34]. The Viterbi algorithm is the more popular of the two and is a maxi-

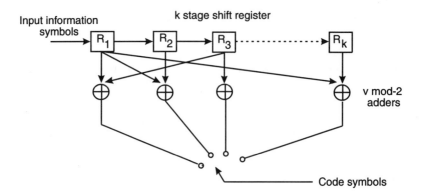

FIGURE 4.3 A simple convolutional encoder.

mum likelihood decoder; i.e., the received sequence is compared with every possible code sequence. The decoding process is achieved by a code trellis. Code trellises become very large and complex as the length of the shift register, k, increases. In fact, the complexity of the Viterbi algorithm is an exponential function of the code's constraint length. The theory of convolutional codes and the various decoding algorithms are mature and are further detailed in [1,4–6].

4.8 APPLICATIONS OF CONVOLUTIONAL CODES

Convolutional encoding, originally developed for deep-space communications [35,36], has also found applications in mobile communications. More recently, convolutional encoding has been implemented in digital cellular systems for the protection of speech [37,38]. We have included an example of convolutional encoding for digital cellular systems, which also illustrates the degree of complexity of a robust coding algorithm for digital mobile radio applications.

In the European digital cellular system, global system for mobile communications (GSM), 1/2 rate convolutional encoding is used in addition to a block code [38–40]. This technique of encoding where two different types of codes are used is known as a concatenated coding scheme [3]. Figure 4.4 illustrates the coding procedure. Data from the speech coder, which uses the residual pulse excited linear predictive (RPE-LTP) coding algorithm, are sent in bursts of 260 bits every 20 ms for error-control coding. The 260 bits are delivered in order of decreasing importance and can be categorized into class 1 (182 bits) and class 2 (78 bits) bits. The first 50 class 1 bits are coded with a (53,50) block code for error detection. The purpose of the three parity bits is to detect errors that are present in the class 1 bits, as they are the most important bits. It has been found that any errors that remain in these bits give rise to such poor speech quality that it is better for the speech decoder to extrapolate the output speech signal based on previous speech frames rather than to use the errored frames. These bits are then combined with the remaining 132 bits. The 185 bits (50 + 3 + 132) are then reordered and appended with 4 tail bits (to reset the convolutional encoder) and the total of 189 bits are fed into the convolutional encoder, which performs a half-rate convolutional code with a constraint length of 5, CC(2,1,5). The 378 coded bits output from the encoder are then appended with the remaining 78 class 2 bits, which have been found to not require protection, to give a total of $2 \times 189 + 78 = 456$ bits every 20 ms, equivalent to a data rate of 22.8 Kbps. The data stream is then block interleaved (described in the following section) over eight frames before transmission over the radio link.

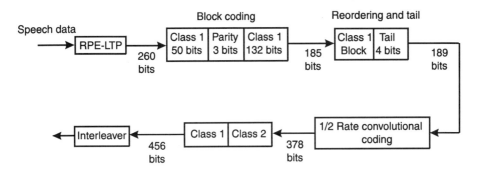

FIGURE 4.4 GSM channel coding—an application of convolutional encoding.

4.9 ENHANCING THE PERFORMANCE OF BLOCK AND CONVOLUTIONAL CODES

The performance of block and convolutional codes in the mobile radio channel is often enhanced by a technique known as interleaving. In a typical communications system, the interleaver is often placed between the FEC encoder and the modulator. Most block and convolutional codes are designed to combat random independent errors, which occur in a memoryless or Gaussian channel. However, for channels with memory, such as the mobile radio channel, burst errors are observed to be dependent on signal transmission impairments (fading, Doppler, etc.). The technique of interleaving is intended to disperse burst errors encountered when the received signal is in a fade. This effectively reduces the concentration of the errors that must be corrected by the channel code. The aim of the interleaver is to make the channel appear random or memoryless to the decoder.

The principle behind interleaving is to spread the error bursts in time. The transmitting end of the encoded stream is loaded into a rectangular matrix row by row. The bits are then read out column by column for transmission. At the receiver, the received data stream is loaded into a matrix column by column and read row by row into the decoder. Such a matrix is shown in Figure 4.5. The effect of this process is to disperse the error bursts encountered in time. Interleaving is often seen as an effective way of increasing the coding gain by as much as 17 dB for a large interleaver. However, interleaving does suffer from introduction of delay dependent on the level of interleaving. Hence, a compromise must be reached so that delays are minimized.

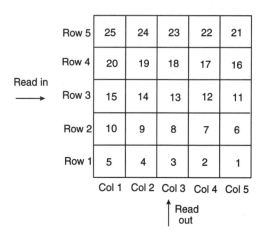

FIGURE 4.5 An interleaving matrix.

4.10 PERFORMANCE OF BLOCK AND CONVOLUTIONAL CODES

The performance of FEC codes is dependent on the error characteristics or mechanisms encountered in the radio channel. Convolutional codes in general possess the advantage of correcting random errors without breaking up the data stream, whereas block codes such as RS are good at correcting both random as well as burst errors, if interleaving is used.

In general, longer codes possess the advantage of better detection in correctable words over shorter codes, hence a higher coding gain can be achieved; however, the penalty is increased complexity and processing delays. For short block codes such as the RS (12,6), a coding gain between 2.5 dB and 18 dB can be achieved in a Rayleigh fading channel of BER 10^{-3} and 10^{-6}, respectively. For a similar code rate with a longer block code of RS (57,29), a coding gain of 7 dB to 29.5 dB can be obtained for the same BER regions [38]. With convolutional codes, soft-decision decoding is also an effective way of increasing the coding gain. In principle, the soft-decision decoding process is demodulator-assisted in the certainty of decisions, based on a confidence interval. In general, for a 1/2 rate convolutional code with a constraint length of 5, the coding gain that can be obtained in a Rayleigh fading channel varies between 0.2 dB (BER 10^{-3}) and 14.5 dB (BER 10^{-6}) with hard-decision decoding and 2.5 dB to 19.8 dB (for the same BER regions) with soft-decision decoding. Interleaving can provide coding gains of as much as 19 dB for hard-decision decoding and 21 dB for soft-decision decoding.

Although the performance of block and convolutional codes have been summarized, it is important to add that the coding gains that can be obtained depend very much on the code rate, channel characteristics (which also depend on the environment—outdoor or indoor), decoding techniques, interleaving depth, etc. It is by no means a firm guideline to the choice of codes but only serves to provide the reader with an idea of the capability and power of the codes.

4.11 AUTOMATIC REPEAT REQUEST SCHEMES

As previously mentioned, ARQ schemes [4,8–11,41] are an alternative form of error control to FEC. The essential difference is that ARQ systems require a feedback channel to inform the transmitter of the success/failure of the retransmission of each block. ARQ schemes can be more reliable than FEC schemes where data applications in the mobile radio channel are concerned. There are three common ARQ protocols in use: *stop and wait (SAW)*, *go back N (GBN)*, and *selective repeat (SR)*. ARQ schemes are often used together with an error detection code, the most common of which is the cyclic redundancy check (CRC). The CRC performs a check on the integrity of the data packet received and signals to the higher layer protocols to initiate an appropriate acknowledgment. FEC codes are also used at times in ARQ systems to perform the error detection (and correction if possible) instead of the CRC. The combination of FEC and ARQ for error detection and correction are more commonly known as *hybrid FEC/ARQ* and will be discussed in the following sections. This section describes the various ARQ schemes available and discusses the advantages/disadvantages of the different techniques and their applicability for mobile data transmission.

4.12 STOP AND WAIT

SAW is the simplest of the ARQ schemes available. The idea behind it is that the transmitter sends a single frame and waits for an acknowledgment. No other frames are transmitted until the receiver replies with a positive acknowledgment (ACK) if the frame received was correct and a negative acknowledgment (NAK) if the frame received was in error. The most attractive feature of SAW ARQ is its simplicity of operation and implementation. However, it has its drawbacks, due to its inefficiency. SAW ARQ is also known as idle RQ because it remains idle waiting for an acknowledgment before the next transmission. The time that the protocol remains idle depends on the propagation delays, transmission times, and protocol processing delays.

Figure 4.6 illustrates the principle behind the SAW ARQ scheme. In the first case, in an error-free transmission, the information frame is appropriately acknowledged and the next frame in sequence is transmitted. In the second case, an information block is corrupted due to transmission errors, and a NAK for that frame is replied. The transmitter, upon receiving a NAK, retransmits the same frame again. Frames and acknowledgments can be lost in transmission and this will hang up the protocol. In order for the protocol to remain efficient, a timer mechanism is required. This is necessary in the third illustration, where an information frame is corrupted and the NAK replied is lost. When the information is initially transmitted, a timer is started and when it expires, the same frame is retransmitted, thus ensuring that the protocol does not hold up. When acknowledgments for correctly received information frames are lost or corrupted, the transmitter resends the frames when the timer expires. However, at the receiver, a duplicate of the frame must be detected, and this is achieved by a sequence number. The last illustration in Figure 4.6 shows this case.

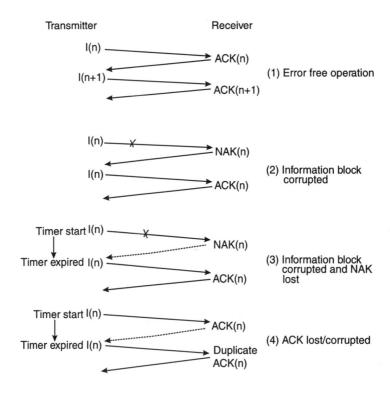

FIGURE 4.6 Stop and wait ARQ.

4.13 CONTINUOUS RQ SYSTEMS

Continuous RQ systems such as go back N and selective repeat send information frames continuously before receiving any acknowledgments. Hence, frames transmitted must be buffered until appropriately acknowledged. It is more efficient than SAW, but there must be a limit on the number of frames transmitted or the buffers will overflow. Therefore, some form of regulation must be introduced. A window is often used to limit the maximum number of frames transmitted. This window (also known as the sliding window) is essentially a buffer containing a list of frames waiting to be acknowledged (the retransmission list). The description of the window mechanism will be clearer as we go through the continuous RQ protocols.

4.13.1 Go Back N

In GBN ARQ, the transmitter may send a series of frames determined by the window size (which is often negotiated during a call setup). Upon detection of an error, the receiver replies with a NAK and will discard all future (new) incoming frames until the frame in error is correctly received. The transmitter, upon receiving a NAK, retransmits the frame in error plus the succeeding frames. Sequence numbers are also part of continuous RQ systems, to detect for duplicates and also to maintain an ordered delivery of frames. Timers are also incorporated in the transmitter, to initiate retransmissions upon expiration (when a NAK is lost, for example). Retransmissions can also be initiated by sending a NAK in the reverse channel. When retransmissions are performed, all outstanding blocks (shown in the ascending queue in Figure 4.7) are retransmitted. The size of the buffer at the receiver is one frame, as it contains the sequence number of the next expected block to keep the order. It will discard all blocks following an errored block until the block is correctly received.

The scheme implemented is the go back N protocol with a window of 7 frames. The *buffers* at the top of the figure indicate the frames in queue waiting to be transmitted in ascending order (note the ordered sequence). An error in the transmission is indicated by "E" and the presence of errors in the return channel is indicated by a dashed line. The round trip delay (processing and transmission delays) in the example is 4 frames. The ACK numbers are acknowledgment sequence numbers, and "?" indicates an acknowledgment corrupted. In the example in Figure 4.7, when the receiver detects a block in error (block 3), a NAK for that block is sent to the transmitter, which triggers the retransmission of blocks 3, 4, 5, and 6. Note that NAK 3 also acknowledges block 2 in the queue (i.e., it acknowledges all blocks prior to this). When an out-of-sequence block is received, shown at the receiver when block 3 is expected but blocks 4, 5, and 6 arrive, the receiver replies with an ACK for the latest correctly received block—in this case 2. GBN schemes generate many wasteful transmissions, as can be seen when an out-of-sequence series of blocks arrives and is discarded because the blocks are out of sequence rather than because they contain errors. Therefore, GBN is not a very efficient protocol.

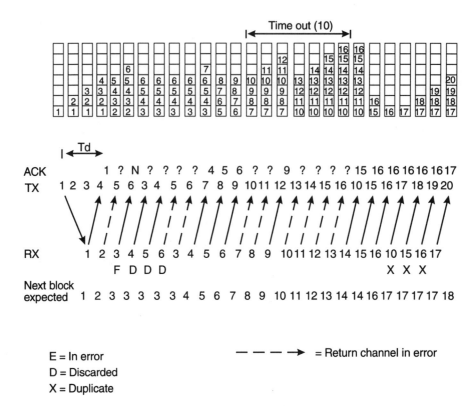

FIGURE 4.7 The go back N protocol.

4.13.2 Selective Repeat

SR is another continuous RQ scheme, where blocks are continuously transmitted. This ARQ technique, unlike GBN, accepts blocks out of sequence but reorders and delivers the received blocks in sequence to the higher layers. Timers are also used in the SR scheme, but during retransmissions, which can be initiated by a NAK received or a time out for a particular block, only that block is retransmitted, unlike GBN. The receiver buffer stores out-of-sequence blocks in the buffer, so that when an in-sequence block arrives, it can be relayed to the higher layers. Hence, buffering is an essential requirement to the SR protocol, with buffers at both ends of the link, unlike GBN. Figure 4.8 illustrates an example of the SR scheme.

The notations used in the illustration are similar to the figure illustrating GBN. In Figure 4.8, block number 1 is received correctly but block 2 is in error, hence, a NAK is forwarded for block 2 requesting retransmission. During this time, blocks 3 and 4 are also sent, due to the round trip delay, however, they need to be buffered for ordered delivery. The receiver now acknowledges continuously the last

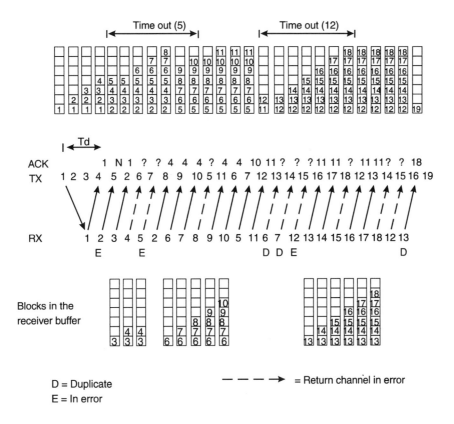

FIGURE 4.8 The selective repeat protocol.

correctly received block, i.e. block 1. When block 2 arrives at the receiver, blocks 2, 3, and 4 are then delivered and the acknowledgment for block 4 is returned, which also acknowledges blocks 2, 3, and 4.

4.14 PERFORMANCE OF ARQ SCHEMES

One can observe almost immediately that the SAW ARQ system is the most inefficient due to the idle periods introduced by the protocol. It is, however, the simplest to implement, with minimal buffer requirements. SAW ARQ yields reasonable throughput if the data transmission rate is low and the round trip delay is small. However, for applications such as satellite systems, where propagation delays are around 500 ms, the delays can be intolerable. GBN achieves better performance due to its continuous nature. However, the performance of GBN is limited by the channel error rate. In the radio channel, where error rates are high, the increase in retransmissions due to errored blocks results in large numbers of duplicates, decreasing the efficiency of the protocol. This will be further illustrated in the later sections.

SR yields the highest throughput of all the protocols due to its efficient use of the channel bandwidth, at the expense of extensive buffering at the receiver and more complex logic at the transmitter and receivers. It has been incorporated in the European DECT standard for data transmission [42] and will be detailed in the later sections.

The analysis of the performance of ARQ protocols are further detailed in [41,43]. Simulations of the ARQ protocols for radio channels are also detailed in [44–47].

4.15 HYBRID ARQ

Yet another category of error-control schemes is the hybrid ARQ. It is the result of the combination of FEC and ARQ schemes [8,48]. The purpose of FEC is to reduce the frequency of retransmissions by correcting error patterns that frequently occur, such as small error bursts. When a large burst of errors occur, it is then left to the ARQ mechanisms to pass the information across the channel.

Hybrid ARQ schemes can be categorized into type 1 and 2 schemes [15]. The aim of type 1 schemes is to detect and correct the data using the FEC. When a codeword is detected to be in error, the receiver attempts to correct the errors. However, if the error pattern is uncorrectable (such as a large burst), the receiver discards the received codeword and sends a request for a retransmission. The same codeword previously sent is then retransmitted. In a type 1 hybrid ARQ scheme, the amount of parity check bits is higher than that of a pure ARQ scheme, as it is required to perform correction as well as detection—unlike conventional ARQ. Hence, when the channel error rate is low, type 1 hybrid ARQ systems will be inefficient, carrying unnecessary overheads. However, when the error rates are high, they have the advantage over pure ARQ systems through reduced retransmissions due to the FEC. Type 1 hybrid ARQ schemes are most suited for channels with a fairly constant level of noise—i.e., a stationary or nonvarying BER. This is because enough error correction can be embedded into the system to correct most of the error patterns encountered, reducing a great deal of retransmission. However, when the channel BER is varying, type 1 hybrid ARQ begins to suffer due to its inflexibility in coping with varying BER.

Type 2 hybrid ARQ, on the other hand, is basically an adaptive hybrid ARQ system, adapting to the channel characteristics. When the channel is good, the system behaves like a pure ARQ system, with only parity-check bits for error detection. This minimizes overheads. When the channel degrades, extra parity bits are included to cope with the change in BER. Hence, the first transmission is coded with parity-check bits for error detection only. When the receiver detects the presence of errors, the word in error is stored in a buffer, and a retransmission is requested. The retransmission is not the original codeword; rather, it is a block of parity-check bits, constructed from the original message, protected with an error correcting code. Upon reception, the parity bits are then used to correct the errors of the erroneous word in the buffer. If correction is not successful, a second retransmission is requested, which may be a repetition of the original codeword or another block of parity-check bits, depending on the algorithm adopted.

4.16 SELECTION AND CHOICE OF ERROR CONTROL CODES

We have outlined and covered the various error-control techniques, such as FEC, ARQ, and hybrid ARQ. FEC codes are very suitable for channels with a consistent BER, as FEC codes are designed optimally for a range of BER. Hence, for the mobile radio channel, FEC alone may be unsuitable and may require additional error control such as ARQ for data reliability. In the selection of an error-control scheme suitable for radio channels, consideration must be given to the requirements of the system or service. The following paragraphs outline several key points in the choice and suitability of an error-control technique for an application.

The most important criterion in the selection of an error-control technique is the application involved and the level of protection required. For voice applications, the error tolerance of the speech data is high compared to data. Error bursts in the radio channel may be interpreted as "clicks" and "pops," but the situation is different with data. Even for data, applications such as video are able to tolerate error bursts to some extent. Images may have regions of black spots but the overall information or image remains intelligible. However, for pure data, such as file transfers or electronic mail, errors in the data may render the transmission useless due to the corruption of crucial information, such as the header. Hence, the transmission of data may require additional parity-check bits to ensure data reliability. The introduction of lower rate codes may be useful for error correction, but we must also consider the overheads involved. This brings us to the next issue, data rates.

In mobile communications, compromise is a must. Implementing a low-rate code to ensure data reliability may result in the user data rate being unbearably low, due to excessive overhead. On the other hand, using a high-code rate may leave too many errors in the data stream uncorrected. Hence, in order to strike a compromise, the system or channel aspects need to be considered. In the previous chapter, the mobile radio propagation environment was described and transmission impairments such as multipath fading, time-selective fading, and frequency-selective fading were considered. The error mechanisms in the channel must be studied so that a suitable error control can be designed. In the outdoor mobile radio channel, where the signal goes through fast fading, the signal fluctuates very rapidly. This results in short error bursts due to the relatively short fade duration. Hence, FEC may be applicable to correct the smaller error bursts, leaving the larger bursts for the ARQ. As previously mentioned, with data transmission over the analog cellular system, RS FEC is used as well with ARQ. However, for the portable radio channel, where the mobile moves at a relatively slow speed, the signal undergoes slow fading. That is, the signal fluctuates less often with the portable radio channel than with the mobile radio channel, and the portable channel's fade duration is longer. As a result, larger error bursts occur. For example, in the indoor radio channel, it has been observed that FEC is not suitable due to the large error bursts that and ARQ should be used instead [47,49]. Fading characteristics must therefore be carefully assessed in the radio channel in order to design a suitable error-control code.

Another factor is the coding delays due to FEC, which can be a disadvantage. FEC schemes suffer from encoding and decoding delays, which increase with size of the block or constraint length, depending on the code. High-speed digital signal processors may be needed, which could consume a lot of power and have an effect on battery life in portable applications. The delays due to interleaving also must be considered if implemented.

ARQ, on the other hand, suffers most from the round trip propagation delays—the time required for the receiver to process the block and transmit an acknowledgment. In a poor-quality channel, it may take several retransmissions to get a block of data across. This is probably not a problem for asynchronous or delay-tolerant applications, but for synchronous or minimum-delay applications, data may have to be delivered to the higher layers with some errors. Hence, it is also important to define the type of services required. These could be a fixed throughput service for synchronous applications or variable throughput service for asynchronous applications.

Other obvious factors that must also be taken into consideration include cost and implementation complexity, but these item will not be covered in this chapter.

4.17 CONCLUSIONS

This chapter has covered the various error-control techniques available and their applicability to the mobile radio channel for data communications. Various FEC and ARQ techniques have been introduced and the advantages and disadvantages of the various techniques have also been discussed. In addition, the performance of FEC and ARQ have been discussed. Detailed analyses have not been included due to the scope of this book, but relevant references have been specified.

With every mobile communications service, it is important that an appropriate error-control scheme be chosen. Factors that must be considered, such as applications, type of service, and channel characteristics, have also been discussed.

References

[1]   Clark, G.C. Jr., and J.B. Cain, *Error Correction Coding for Digital Communications*, New York: Plenum Press, 1981.
[2]   McEliece, R.J., *Theory of Information Theory and Coding*, Reading, MA: Addison Wesley, 1977.
[3]   Sweeney, P., *Error Control Coding: An Introduction*, Englewood Cliffs, NJ: Prentice Hall, 1991.

[4]   Lin, S., and D. Costello, Jr., *Error Control Coding: Fundamentals and Applications*, Englewood Cliffs, NJ: Prentice Hall, 1983.

[5]   Blahut, R.E., *Theory and Practice of Error Control Codes*, Reading, MA: Addison Wesley, 1983.

[6]   Blahut, R.E., *Principles and Practice of Information Theory*, Reading, MA: Addison Wesley, 1983.

[7]   Bhargava, K., "Forward Error Correction Schemes for Digital Communications," *IEEE Communications Magazine*, Jan. 1983, pp. 11–19.

[8]   Lin, S., D.J. Costello, Jr., and M. Miller, "Automatic-Repeat-Request Error Control Schemes," *IEEE Communications Magazine*, Vol. 22, No. 12, Dec. 1984, pp. 5–17.

[9]   Tanenbaum, A.S., *Computer Networks*, Englewood Cliffs, NJ: Prentice Hall, 1988.

[10] Halsall, F., *Data Communications, Computer Networks and Open Systems*, Third Edition, Reading, MA: Addison Wesley, 1992.

[11] Stallings, W., *Data and Computer Communications*, Third Edition, New York: Maxwell Macmillan, 1991.

[12] Sklar, B., *Digital Communications—Fundamentals and Applications*, Englewood Cliffs, NJ: Prentice Hall, 1988.

[13] Blahut, R.E., *Digital Transmission of Information*, Reading, MA: Addison Wesley, 1990.

[14] Berlekamp, E.R., "The Technology of Error Correcting Codes," *Proceedings of IEEE*, Vol. 68, May 1980, pp. 564–593.

[15] Berlekamp, E.R., R.E. Peile, and S.P. Pope," The Application of Error Control to Communications," *IEEE Communications Magazine*, Vol. 25, No. 4, April 1987, pp. 44–57.

[16] Berlekamp, E.R. (ed.), *Key Papers in the Development of Coding Theory*, IEEE Press, 1973.

[17] Chien, R.T., "Block Coding Techniques for Reliable Data Transmission," *IEEE Transactions on Communications*, COM-19, Oct. 1971, pp. 743–751.

[18] Sharpe, Tony K. "Paging Systems" in *Personal and Mobile Radio Systems*, Macario, R.C.V. (ed.), London: Peter Peregrinus, 1991.

[19] Sandvos, J.L., "A Comparison of Binary Paging Codes," *Proceedings IEEE Vehicular Technology Conference 82*, May 1982.

[20] Mabey, P.J., "Digital Signalling for Radio Paging," *IEEE Transactions on Vehicular Technology*, Vol. VT-30, May 1981.

[21] Flack, M., and M. Gronow, *Cellular Communications for Data Transmission*, NCC Blackwell, 1990.

[22] Ito et al., "Facsimile Signal Transmission in Digital Mobile Radio," *Proceedings IEEE VTC 88*, June 15–17, 1988, pp. 83–88.

[23] Department of Trade and Industry/Radio Communications Agency (UK), "Common Air Interface Specification to be Used for the Interworking Between Cordless Telephone Apparatus including Public Access Service," MPT 1375, London, May 1989.

[24] Tuttlebee, W., *Cordless Telecommunications in Europe*, Springer Verlag, 1991.

[25] Tuttlebee, W., "Cordless Personal Communications," *IEEE Communications Magazine*, Vol. 30, No. 12, December 1992, pp. 42–53.

[26] Gardiner, John, "The Telepoint System," in *Personal and Mobile Radio Systems*, Macario, R.C.V. (ed.), London: Peter Peregrinus, 1991.

[27] Jalali, A., G. Mony, and L. Strawczynski, "Performance of Data Protocols for In-Building Wireless Systems," *Proceedings IEEE International Conference on Universal Personal Communications*, Ottawa, Canada, 1992, pp. 15.02.1–5.

[28] ETSI, Draft European Telecommunications Standard 300-131, Valbonne, France, 1991.

[29] Wong, "The Performance of the CT2 System for Data Services," *Proc. IEEE Vehicular Technology Conference 1994*, Stockholm, Sweden, June 7–11, 1994.

[30] Blahut, R.E., "A Universal Reed Solomon Decoder," *IBM Journal of Research & Development*, Vol. 28, No. 2, March 1984, pp. 150–158.

[31] Arambepola, B., and S. Choomchuay, "Algorithms and Architectures for Reed Solomon Codes," *GEC Journal of Research*, Vol. 9, No. 3, 1992, pp. 172–184.

[32] Choomchuay, S., and B. Arambepola, "Time Domain Algorithms and Architectures for Reed Solomon Decoding," *IEE Proceedings I*, Vol. 140, No. 3, London, June 1993, pp. 189–194.

[33] Blahut, R.E., *Algebraic Methods for Signal Processing and Communications Coding*, Springer Verlag, 1992.

[34] Forney, G.D., Jr., "The Viterbi Algorithm," *Proceedings IEEE*, Vol. 61, No. 3, March 1973, pp. 268–278.

[35] Forney, G.D., Jr., "Coding and its Applications in Space Communications," *IEEE Spectrum*, June 1970, pp. 47–58.

[36] Viterbi, A.J., "Convolutional Codes and their Performance in Communications Systems," *IEEE Transactions on Communications Technology*, COM-19, Oct. 1971, pp. 772–781.

[37] Miya, K., O. Kato, and K. Honma, "Design of Error Correction Methods Using Redundancy of Speech Coder Data," *Proc. IEEE VTC*, 1992, pp. 176–182.

[38] Steele, R., *Mobile Radio Communications*, London: Pentech Press, 1992.

[39] Hodges, M.R.L., "The GSM Radio Interface," *British Telecom Technology Journal*, Vol. 8, No. 1, January 1990.

[40] ETSI/TC, "Channel Coding," GSM Recommendation 05.03, Valbonne, France, February 1992.

[41] Comroe, R.A., and D.J. Costello, Jr., "ARQ Schemes for data transmission in Mobile Radio Systems," *IEEE J-SAC-2* No. 4, Vol. 2, July 1984.

[42] ETSI, *Digital European Cordless Telecommunications Common Interface Part 4: Data Link Control Layer*, ETS 300 175-4, Valbonne, France, October 1992.

[43] Saeki, B.H., and I. Rubin, "An Analysis of a TDMA Channel Using Stop-and-Wait, Block, and Select-and-Repeat ARQ Error Control," *IEEE Transactions on Communications*, COM-30, No. 5, May 1982, pp. 1162–1173.

[44] Chang, L.F., "Throughput Estimation of ARQ Protocols for Rayleigh Fading Channel," *Proceedings of the ICC '90*, Atlanta, pp. 335.6.1–6.

[45] Chang, L.F, and P.T. Porter, "Data Services in a TDMA, Digital Portable Radio System," IEEE Conference Record CH2827-4/90/000-0480, Globecom '90, pp. 404.2.1–5.

[46] Chuang, J.C.I., "Comparison of Two ARQ protocols in a Rayleigh Fading Environment," *Proceedings of IEEE VTC '90*, pp. 571–575.

[47] Wong, P., and F. Halsall, "Data Applications for DECT," *Proc. IEEE International Conference on Communications*, Geneva, Switzerland, May 23–26, 1993, pp. 49.5.1–5.

[48] Leung, C.S.K., and A. Lam, "Forward Error Correction for an ARQ System," *IEEE Transactions on Communications*, COM-29, No. 10, October 1981, pp. 1,514–1,519.

[49] Owen, F.C., and C.P. Pudney, "DECT—Integrated Services for Cordless Telecommunications," *Proc. 5th IEE International Conference on Mobile Radio and Personal Communications*, Warwick, England, 1989, pp. 152–156.

CHAPTER 5
▼▼▼

DATA OVER PMR/TETRA/DSRR

Until recently, data has been relatively little used in the private mobile radio field. During the past ten years, the use of digital signaling in PMR has gradually increased as the trunked radio market has expanded. Previously, most call setups had been accomplished by operating in open net systems, five-tone signaling (select 5), DTMF, or subaudible-tone signaling (continuous tone-coded signaling system). All of these methods are too slow for the transfer of data.

In the late 1970s, various proprietary signaling protocols started appearing. The most notable was from Motorola, which generated a family of signaling schemes operating between 600 and 4,800 bps. The higher data rates used direct modulation of an FM carrier. At about the same time, Mobile Data International, a Canadian company in Vancouver, was founded specifically to produce data terminal units for use on PMR systems. This firm also used a data rate of 4.8 Kbps, along with a unique direct modulation method. In Europe, several of the national mobile radio trade organizations began to look at nonproprietary solutions. The first to produce an interim standard was ZVEI in Germany, which came up with a protocol operating at 1,200 bps. This protocol has a 40-bit codeword with only 8 bits of redundancy. At almost the same time, a working party of the Electrical Engineering Association in the U.K. commenced working on a similar project. This culminated in a recommendation adopted by the U.K. Radiocommunications Agency, which became known as MPT 1317. Subsequently, a very similar standard was published in France with minor differences in the word synchronization frame and a requirement that the modulation have a phase (PM) rather than frequency (FM) characteristic. This standard is known as PAA 1382.

The common feature of these European standards is that they all use subcarrier modulation and fast frequency shift keying (FFSK). (PAA 1382 requires that symbol transitions occur at the peak of the signal, whereas other systems require that they occur at the zero crossing point). Subcarrier modulation was used to enable the retrospective fitting of digital signaling to existing systems. This was achieved by direct connection to the microphone and speaker circuits of the radios. The standard data rate of 1,200 bps was chosen because the spectrum occupancy of the signal is compatible with the available bandwidth in both 12.5 and 25 kHz separated systems. Another advantage, as seen by the manufacturers, was that the occupied bandwidth of the signaling was also compatible with private wire telephone circuits, which many PMR systems use for connection to hilltop sites, so it did not require the use of additional modems.

5.1 THE MPT 1317 AND PAA 1382 STANDARDS

Both of these standards consist of a 64-bit codeword preceded by 32 bits of synchronization, the first 16 bits of which enable clock synchronization of the receiver and the next 16 are for frame (word) synchronization.

16 bits	16 bits	48 bits	16 bits
Bit sync.	Frame sync.	Data	CRC

FIGURE 5.1 MPT 1317 frame structure.

The clock synchronization is achieved by the transmission of alternate ones and zeros. The frame synchronization is a unique bit sequence. In the case of MPT 1317, it is C4D7 H, and for PAA 1382 it is B433 H. In subsequent standards, the complements are also used to denote signaling on channels other than that used for control. The French synchronization sequence exhibits a better balanced auto correlation function and, it is claimed, a better chance of correction should there be any bit errors. There is, however, an argument that any attempts to correct the word synchronization should not be made (to any signaling codeword). This argument is based on the premise that if a call can be set up only by the use of error correction to improve the signaling channel performance, then it is likely that the quality of the traffic channel is too poor for reasonable communication. This may be true for many single-site PMR systems, where the control and traffic channels are colocated, but in larger, more intelligent systems with handover, it may be possible to find a more suitable traffic channel after the mobile has established contact with the system. Also, the errors introduced may have been of a transient nature—for example, ignition interference from a passing vehicle—and by the time the communication session commences, the traffic channel is "clean". Therefore, the decision to use or not to use error correction on a signaling channel is not clear and must be taken in light of the particular system and its architecture.

Messages are contained in 64-bit codewords using a (63,48) BCH cyclic block code with an additional parity bit. The 16-bit CRC (cyclic redundancy check) is calculated from the following polynomial:

$$x^{15} + x^{14} + x^{11} + x^4 + x^2 + 1$$

The final bit of the BCH word is inverted and the overall parity is made to be odd. This form of codeword, in conjunction with hard-decision decoding, allows the detection of all odd numbers of errors, any 5 errors, and any burst error up to a length of 16. [1] The falsing probability per message is approximately 2 in 10^{-6}. In the case of the shorter ZVEI eight-bit CRC, the falsing probability has been shown to be around 4 in 10^{-4} [2]. It has been shown that it is possible to use the CRC to correct as well as detect errors, and with soft-decision decoding up to 5 random bits or any burst up to 16 bits can be corrected [1]. However, this can lead to a much higher falsing rate and in a signaling/data system, this may well be unacceptable. As shown earlier in Chapter 4, the best solution is to *wrap* the codeword in either a convolution or block code and maintain the security of the full CRC. Again, however, there may be situations where it is not possible to add the additional coding at source. If the integrity of the data is not critical, it may be acceptable to increase the system gain at the receiver by error correction using the CRC.

Neither of the two standards define the use of the 48 data bits. This has to be left to the end user. However, subsequent standards MPT 1327/43 and PAA 2424 volumes 1 and 2 have defined their use and have become de facto signaling standards in Europe and many parts of the world for analog trunked radio systems. Again the U.K. and French standards are very similar and differ only in the detail of the numbering schemes.

MPT 1327 defines the functionality of the fields within the codeword, and MPT 1343 defines the use of specified codewords when applied to signaling in a trunked radio system. A particular feature of the standard is the ability to send short data messages on the control channel in addition to the signaling. Thus, although it is primarily used to set up calls in an analog trunked network, the control channel has the ability to send free-form data in a maximum of four concatenated codewords, in addition to the transfer of status messages. The status message is a number between 0 and 31. The short data message may be free-format data of up to 184 bits or 25 ASCII characters. More recently, extended data messaging has been introduced on the control channel. It allows up to 704 free-format data bits or 100 ASCII characters to be sent. The short data message is now referred to as single segment transactions (SST) and the extended data as multiple segment transactions (MST).

Standard data are specified for use on a dedicated channel and are of packet-switched format at a defined rate of 1,200 bps. There is an option for customized higher data rates. The use of nonprescribed data on traffic channels is allowed within the MPT 1343 standard. The nonprescribed data are not restricted to the 1200 bps rate. Nonprescribed data are allowed higher data rates up to 4.8 Kbps, as long as the modulation method does not contravene the limits set in I-ETS 300 113 [3], which has been defined by ETSI. Work still continues on the MPT standard, with participation from many European and Scandinavian countries.

5.2 INDIRECTLY MODULATED NONTRUNKED RADIO STANDARDS

As mentioned earlier, the MPT 1317/27/43 standards have become the de facto standard in Europe. However, these standards were aimed at the trunked radio market and no similar standard emerged for normal nontrunked PMR use until ECTEL (the European Manufacturers' Association) produced their own version. This, with some modification, has been accepted by ETSI and is known as BIIS 1200 (binary interchange of information and signaling) [4]. The same codeword structure as in MPT 1317 is used. The frame synchronization word is the same as that used in PA 1382 but with optional phase or frequency modulation characteristics. Additional convolution coding is recommended for forward error correction, and the use of specific data compression techniques is advised for the transmission of long data messages.

This standard supports many services and facilities, including selective and group calling, broadcast and emergency calls, repeater access, PSTN and PABX access, and status and data transmissions. The data protocol is based on the HDLC protocol as defined in ISO 4335 [5]. Three modes of data exchange are supported:

- Asynchronous balanced mode (ABM);
- Group mode (GM);
- Asynchronous disconnected mode (ADM).

These are defined as follows:

ABM is the data link operational mode in which both stations of a point-to-point configuration may initiate, cancel, or terminate a data transmission spontaneously. Therefore, both stations utilize the same commands and responses.

GM is the data link operational mode in which one station may initiate, cancel, or terminate a data transmission to several stations simultaneously in an unbalanced mode whereby the coordinating control is the initiating station. Only the initiating station may transmit data packets.

ADM is the data link nonoperational mode in which a station is logically disconnected from the data link and can neither transmit nor accept numbered commands or responses.

Three data services are supported:

Acknowledged point-to-point operation is used for multiple information packet transmission in a balanced mode. The information transfer is acknowledged at the data-link level. Error recovery, packet sequence integrity, and flow control are defined.

Acknowledged broadcast operation is used for limited multiple information packet transmission in an unbalanced mode. The information transfer is acknowledged at the data-link level under control of the initiating station by a polling mechanism. Error recovery, packet sequence integrity, and flow control are defined.

Unacknowledged operation is used for point-to-point or broadcast single (unnumbered) information packet transmission. No error recovery and no flow control is defined at the data-link level.

If data compression is used, it must conform to the RADIX 40 method, which is based on CCITT International Alphabet No. 5.

Because of a perceived need for further standardization to stimulate the market, a group of international manufacturers has formed an ad hoc group called the User Access Definition Group (UADG) to build on the success of these nonproprietary standards for the wider use of data transfer in the trunked and nontrunked PMR market. A specification has been drawn up, which defines the interface between a mobile radio and a data-terminal equipment and is known as MAP 27 (Mobile Access Protocol for MPT 1327) [6]. The physical interface is in accordance with RS 232 and CCITT rec. V.28 and operates at a nominal 9.6 Kbps (with a preferred option of 1,200 bps). It uses asynchronous data transfer of eight-bit characters with single start and stop bits. The transactions between the terminal equipment and the mobile radio interface are fully duplex, even if the radio is operating simplex. The structure is based on the ISO seven-layer reference model for open systems interconnection (OSI) and layers 1, 2, and 3 are defined in the standard. The higher application layers are not included. The network layer has been designed to complement the MPT 1327/43 signaling protocols to minimize buffer storage and processing complexity by using, where possible, comparable codewords. It may also be used for data transfer and control of the radio with other data transfer schemes such as BIIS 1200.

5.3 DIRECT MODULATED SYSTEMS

During the 1980s, most of the mobile radios in production could not support direct modulation without modification. Motorola was one of the exceptions as that company was also producing equipment suitable for digital speech encryption, which required a similar interface. The encrypted radios operated at a data rate of 12 Kbps in a 25-kHz separated channel but used digital signaling for call setup at 3.6 Kbps. The signaling scheme was used in the Smartnet analog trunked systems in a similar way as MPT 1327 was used in Europe. Subsequently, 4.8 Kbps was incorporated and the latest products use 9.6 Kbps and multilevel modulation, as in the RD-LAP protocol (see chapter 7). At around the same time, MDI entered the market place with an add-on data product, which also used direct modulation but which had a novel modulation scheme that required minimal modification to the basic speech radio. The competing systems used different protocols, known as MDC4800 (mobile data communications protocol) from Motorola and MMP4800 (mobile message protocol) from MDI. Ultimately, MDI were acquired by Motorola and the MMP product was discontinued.

5.3.1 MMP4800

The original MDI system supported many different channel access methods dependent on the use to which the data scheme was to be put. If it were a fully duplex scheme then digital sense multiple access (DSMA) would be used. Under no load conditions, the base station sends an *idle* tone, which consists of a repeated pattern of "11000001100000." Every two seconds a synchronizing message is transmitted to allow mobiles to obtain byte synchronism with the base station. The data is formatted into seven-bit frames but only six of the bits are used for data. The remaining bit is designated the busy bit and is set or reset by the detection of incoming data at the base station. Thus, should there be an incoming message, the outbound idle message becomes "11001001100100," which is repeated until the inbound channel becomes clear or there are outbound messages to be sent.

If operation is through a repeater or single frequency simplex then carrier sense multiple access (CSMA) is the preferred method. The squelch output of the receiver is used as the means to inhibit the unit transmitting. Unfortunately, many of the cheaper receivers have a long squelch hang time and a poor attack time, so the data system is much less efficient than when DSMA is used. A compromise has been used in which a data detector has replaced the squelch circuit for control purposes. This can be made to operate much faster and reduce the window of opportunity for contention. Slotted aloha systems have been installed but have been found not to offer as great a level of efficiency as the other methods if the traffic density is high. In terms of radio interfacing, they are simpler, as no RSSI function is required, and have been used in systems with a low probability of message collisions. An interesting feature of the implementation of MDI is that, unlike other systems where each mobile is required to generate a random number to determine its access slot, the mobile population is split into groups, each of which has an assigned slot. Although this spreads the chances of a collision within the total population, it does not randomize access sufficiently and leaves a significant chance of contention within a group if they are all active at the same time in the same area.

The modulation method is unusual in that data "ones" are represented by either a positive or negative excursion of a half cycle of a 2.4 kHz tone and a logical "zero" by an unmodulated carrier.

This form of modulation has the advantage of allowing only two possible states, either deviating or not deviating. When applied to the carrier, the 2.4-kHz half waves are alternated between positive and negative polarity so there is no possi-

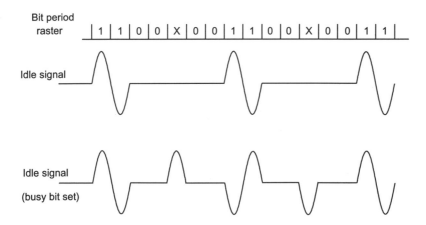

FIGURE 5.2 MMP signal modulation.

bility of a residual dc component remaining in the recovered signal received at the discriminator. This also means that the complexity of dual point modulation at the transmitter synthesizer is avoided and dc coupling is unnecessary at the receiver. The disadvantage is that because the "one, zero, one" transitions occur at the zero crossing point of the modulation; they occur at the point of maximum gradient and thus produce significant sidebands. These must be removed before transmission with a 5-kHz low-pass filter, and a receiver of sufficient bandwidth and low group delay must be employed to allow accurate reconstruction. Other modulation schemes for the same data rate are able to contain the sideband power more compactly but without the simplicity.

The MMP4800 radio channel protocol is unusual in that majority-bit voting is used as a means of error correction in the message headers. The header is sent three times and a composite header generated from the result of a majority vote taking each corresponding bit in turn. The resultant header is error checked using a block-parity check. Alternate transmissions of the header are sent inverted for additional protection. The main message part is broken down into blocks of 45 characters. These blocks are encoded for transmission using a (63, 45) Reed Solomon code for FEC.(see Chapter 4) With this level of coding, it is possible to correct up to 17% of the total error content of a block. The largest message contains eight text block (360 characters). ARQ is used to resend data that are impossible to correct.

5.3.2 MDC4800

The MDC method employs straightforward FSK modulation and requires th modulator and discriminator have a good low-frequency response. The data th ganized so that the effects of a dc offset are minimized and the required ba low-is from about 3 Hz to 3 kHz. Normally a deviation of 50% of the maximu able in the channel is used in order to meet the regulatory requirements of adjacent channel power. The modulation is polarity-sensitive and cannot be decoded if it should become inverted. This means that each radio type must have its architecture verified before use in a specific data system, as data can be easily inverted in the receiver mixing process. The convention for MDC4800 is that a data "1" is represented by a positive frequency offset and a data "0" is represented by a negative offset.

The over-air protocol is quite complex and uses different-length headers for different-length messages. All headers are preceded by a 4-byte processor header, which defines the message handling and sequencing. An additional 6-byte header is used for outbound short fixed-length messages; an 8-byte header, for long variable-length messages; and an 11-byte header, for long fixed-length messages. The 8-byte header is additionally accompanied by a 7-byte application header, which precedes messages of between 1 to 1,920 bytes of data.

The message preamble is made up 20 bits of alternating ones and zeros for bit synchronization followed by a 40-bit word synchronization pattern. No error correction is used, but if at least 35 of the last 40 bits received match the word synchronization pattern, then word synchronization is detected. The data blocks when encoded consist of 112 bits and are made up of 48 information bits, 56 error-correction bits, and eight channel state bits. There are three types of data blocks. The *command block* and *general data block* are further protected by subdividing the information into 32 data bits and a 16-bit CRC. The *text block* consists of six bytes of text. The 48 information bits from any type of block have a further eight channel-state bits appended and the resultant 56-bit block is convolution coded to produce a 112-bit code word. Before transmission, this codeword is reordered to an interleaving depth 16, which means that together with the convolution coding and the channel-state bits, consecutive user data bits are 33 bits apart. This minimizes he chances of lost data due to a noise burst on the channel.

The protocols that have been developed for these PMR standards have now 1 further enhanced, and with the addition of suitable infrastructure, they have 1ed the basis of the public data networks, which are described in Chapter 7. At time there are only manufacturers' proprietary standards in general use for di- nodulated data, but in Europe it has been recognized that the route to low-cost ment and expansion of the market is through standardization. The following 1 describes the latest standard emerging from ETSI for use both in private and networks.

TRA

Tra
supp ropean trunked radio (TETRA) is an initiative that started in ETSI and is stand. by the European Union for the introduction of a digital trunked radio not too Work started slowly in 1988 as many manufacturers and operators were en to see yet another trunking standard appear just as they were installing

their first analog systems. The same situation was mirrored in cellular radio, where work on the GSM standards was gathering pace. However, in this instance, a greater need existed as many different analog cellular standards were in use across Europe. Other than proprietary systems, MPT 1327/43 had become ubiquitous, and the need for a new trunking standard was much less. However, the requirement for a *data only* standard did have some priority, and this moved ahead faster than the voice requirement. Manufacturers were requested to make formal proposals to the ETSI subtechnical committee (STC-RES 06) for a digital system, which gave significant spectral efficiency and capacity advantages over current technology. The proposals ranged from single channel narrow band (5-kHz separated) FDMA linear systems to six channels on a 25-kHz separated carrier (TDMA) system using a complex modulation scheme. After considerable deliberations and much discussion, the system finally chosen supports four channels per 25-kHz separated carrier, with an option that it will be possible to support two channels on a 12.5-kHz channel at a future date.

The main characteristics of the air interface are as follows:

Channel separation	25 kHz (12.5 kHz as an option)
Modulation bit rate	36 Kbps (18 kbaud symbol rate)
Number of channels (voice & data)	
V/D system	4 (TDMA)
Modulation	$\pi/4$-DQPSK
Gross bit rate (for packet data optimized system)	28.8 Kbps

The constraints put on the TETRA system are severe in that TETRA is expected to co-exist with current analog PMR radio allocations, and therefore it is required to meet similar adjacent channel power requirements. (A minor relaxation has been allowed in that although TETRA is equivalent to a 25-kHz separated FDMA system, the adjacent channel power limit is the one used for 12.5-kHz channels, i.e., -60 dBc). In analog cellular systems (AMPS and TACS), these requirements are further relaxed because it is possible by correct frequency planning to avoid adjacent channels operating from the same site. In the case of GSM, the adjacent channel power level is even worse but the C/I performance is better, and this makes it possible to plan a spectrally efficient system within a given band of frequencies. However, at the band edges, a guard band is required to protect other, more susceptible systems, which removes some of the advantages gained.

One of the features of the TETRA modulation method is that it requires the RF power amplifiers to operate in a linear mode to avoid spectrum spreading. To this end, the concept of a common linearization channel (CLCH) has been adopted.

5.4.1 Linearization

This logical channel is represented by a time slot that occurs about once every second, during which all active mobiles may transmit a burst to check their own linear operating state. This is performed by transmission of a training sequence, and depending on the transmitter implementation, by adjustment of the feedback parameters to correct the nonlinear error. This error is likely to be at its greatest just after switch on, so even mobiles that are in standby mode may linearize their power amplifiers before transmitting on any logical control or traffic channel. If it is necessary to change frequency in order to find a free traffic channel, the first action of both transmitting or receiving mobiles is to linearize their power amplifiers on the CLCH of the new frequency.

5.4.2 Time-Division Structure

The basic time slot is just over 14 ms long. This is equivalent to 510 bit periods or 255 symbol periods. The length of slot was chosen as a compromise between having minimum delay in the system—a very short slot—or a long delay and the capability of powerful coding and interleaving over the duration of a slot. In GSM, interleaving is over several slots because the slot length is very short. This adds to the complexity of the system. In TETRA, it was decided to make the slot of sufficient duration to be compatible with current speech coder technology and make it possible to interleave over a single slot. The end-to-end speech delay was not considered to be as big a problem as in GSM because the system is weighted towards simplex rather than duplex working. The frame structure is shown in Figure 5.3.

The hyper frame usually consists of 12 multiframes but may be extended to multiple integers of 12 multiframes if required for specific purposes. The uplink (mobile to base station) is synchronized to the down link but offset from it by two time slots. This is to allow a mobile to transmit and receive in the half duplex mode in the same logical channel. If a mobile is a long distance from the base site, the base station is able to detect that the incoming time slots are suffering from a propagation delay. Information is conveyed to the mobile to advance the timing of its transmissions to maintain accurate slot timing at the base station receiver. Not only can the slot timing be maintained very accurately, the mobile transmitting frequency may be locked to the base station to which it is working. This is very important, as the modulation method leaves little room for frequency drift before causing problems of overspill of transmitted power into the adjacent channel. It is also necessary for the received signal to be centered accurately in the middle of the receiver IF filters to avoid problems caused by differential group delay. This could have been solved by imposing very stringent limits on the tolerance of the reference oscillator in the mobiles. This is likely to be a very costly solution, so an alternative method has been built into the protocol. A field has been specified in the down link synchronization burst, which contains a specific code sequence of *ones* and *zeros*. This code sequence synthesizes continuous unmodulated carrier transmission at a frequency

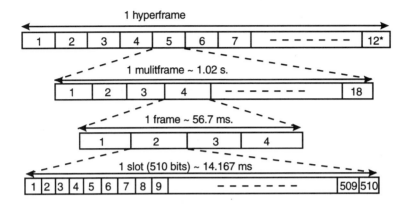

* A hyperframe may be an integer multiple of 12 multiframes
for some special purposes, i.e., encryption.

FIGURE 5.3 TETRA frame structure.

2.25 kHz above the nominal carrier frequency. This sequence may be used to trim
any frequency error in the reference oscillator in the mobile.

5.4.3 Multiple Access

An interesting feature of TETRA is the way in which a mobile is allowed to make
access to the system. In conventional slotted aloha, the number of mobiles that can
be supported by a control channel is limited by the probability of collisions of the
access attempts of different mobiles. It has been shown [7] that only 1/e (36.8%) of
the available access slots are usable. In TETRA the uplink access slots are subdi-
vided into two half slots, thus doubling the probability of gaining access. All subsequent transactions use reserved slots; i.e., other mobiles may not use them for
random access. Although further subdivision of the time slot is possible, simulations
have shown that an even shorter length data message would carry insufficient information for all types of call setup [8]. This means that more reserved slot transactions would be necessary to set up some calls, which would not give optimum usage
of the signaling channel.

5.4.4 Call Setup

If on a given carrier a logical control channel is present, then that channel must oc-
cupy time slot one of the TDMA structure. In a lightly loaded system, where succes-

sive frames may be used in a call setup, then a call may be established in under 100 ms, as is shown in the Figure 5.4.

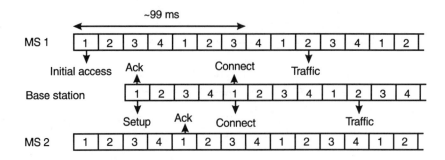

The numbers indicate the time slot of the relevant transmitter.

FIGURE 5.4 Call setup timing.

5.4.5 Error Control

The generic error-control mechanism for the signaling channels is limited by the size of the signaling subblock. Because one of the requirements of TETRA is fast call setup, it was decided that each signaling message would be independent. This means that the interleaving distance is limited to being within the signaling subblock. Each signaling message carries 124 information bits, to which a CRC is added. The generator polynomial takes the well-known CCITT [9] form:

$$g(x) = x^{16} + x^{12} + x^5 + 1$$

The resultant 140 bits are block coded using a 16 state rate-compatible punctured convolution (RCPC) code [10]. Simulations have been performed for a mobile traveling at 50 km/h and using a carrier frequency of 400 MHz (which is where the first TETRA systems are expected to operate). Soft-decision Viterbi decoding was employed, and interleaving was performed over a block of 216 bits. The results showed that the throughput and the grade of service at low signal levels met the requirements expected of the TETRA service [8].

The error-control mechanisms on the traffic channels are not yet finalized as the choice of voice codec to be used, and the level of redundancy for some critical bits must still be determined. However, the use of similar RCPC is envisaged, but with interleaving extending over more than one time slot to improve the performance in a burst-error environment. As mentioned before, this is possible because the TETRA service is aimed primarily at half-duplex operation, and the absolute delay is not as critical as in fully duplex working.

5.4.6 Special Features of the Protocol for Data Transmission

The protocol has been designed so that either voice-plus-data services or data-only services may be supported. In the case of the voice-plus-data usage, data messages will use the time slot structure in the same way as a voice circuit; i.e., it will be a circuit-oriented connection. Slot stealing during a voice transmission will make it possible for the transmission of control messages or slow data transfer between users simultaneously. In the packet data optimized (PDO) mode of operation, it will be possible to concatenate all the traffic timeslots to allow data rates of 19.2 Kbps net or 28.8 Kbps gross. At this time, no agreement to produce a standard format for PDO data transfer has been possible, and it is up to manufacturers to define their own.

5.4.7 Other Features of the Protocol

During transmission, a mobile station must monitor the downlink access information channel to verify that transmit permission has been given for it to transmit in its next uplink slot. This facility allows rapid reassignment of the radio resource. It also offers independent allocation of uplink and associated downlink channels and allows the use of transmission trunking, quasitransmission trunking, and message trunking.

Handover is supported, but is more of a mobile function rather than an infrastructure-determined action. The mobile unit may scan adjacent cells to find a better signal quality. (Because of the time-division nature of the protocol, this can be equally achieved during a call or while monitoring the control channel). Once found, the mobile may either request the current cell to initiate the handover or it may make access to the new cell itself. The former method will give a seamless handover, while the latter will introduce a short discontinuity. The method used is dependent on the complexity of both the infrastructure and the intelligence of the mobile. An event label is used on the air interface to minimize the risk of a crossed connection during the handover or other temporary loss of connection, such as during a fade.

End-to-end encryption is supported by the protocol but is only required in those cases where a serious attack is being made. The use of a radio scanner without sophisticated decoding facilities would not be enough to decode the normal signals. Apart from being digital and time-division multiplexed, the signals are interleaved for transmission and scrambled by the modulo 2 addition of a scrambling sequence, which is variable-dependent on the scrambling length of the message and can take any one of four values. However, should it be needed, a speech or data application may contain its own separate encryption for additional security.

5.4.8 Network Architecture

It is the intention that the TETRA infrastructure should contain as many of the normal line standard features as possible. To this end, most interfaces reflect their equivalent in ISDN or X.25. The radio infrastructure architecture is intended to allow manufacturers to develop their own designs, but any interconnection between systems shall be achieved via the intersystem interface (ISI). This will allow large networks to be assembled from smaller systems designed and built by different manufacturers, and it will allow mobiles to roam freely throughout the network.

5.5 DIGITAL SHORT-RANGE RADIO

DSRR has come a long way since the days of the private advanced radio system (PARS), which was conceived at the EEA during the mid to late 1980s. At that time, a group of British radio manufacturers started on an initiative to produce a new form of PMR radio, which required a minimum of licensing and gave the advantages of trunked radio to a wide variety of potential users. Two megahertz of spectrum at 933–935 MHz had been identified by the DTI for citizen's band use but was not being heavily populated, mainly due to lack of equipment availability at reasonable cost. It was suggested that if a protocol that would allow co-existence with existing users could be produced, such a service would be authorized. A project team was formed and each manufacturer was assigned a particular task in the production of a pair of prototype units. These units were assembled and demonstrated, and computer simulations of the protocol were made. From these simulations, the basic parameters of two control channels supporting 77 traffic channels were developed. One of the interesting features of the trunking method employed is that because a calling mobile must first identify a free traffic channel, the contention on the control channels starts to reduce as the traffic load increases. This is the opposite of what occurs on conventional centrally controlled systems, where contention increases as load increases until instability occurs, unless extra measures are taken. In other words, it is a self-regulating protocol. The simulations also indicated that with a reasonable traffic load expectancy (one call of 30 seconds duration per hour per user), approximately 2,000 users could be supported in the same geographic area, with a mean call setup time of about four seconds.

Concurrent with this work, changes occurred in Europe and ETSI was formed. DSRR was incorporated into the work program of STC RES 03, whose prime responsibility was the production of the DECT standard. It soon became obvious that a separate working group was required for DSRR, so a new subtechnical committee RES 07 was formed. During 1990 a project team worked in the ETSI headquarters at Sophia Antipolis and produced the draft standard I-ETS 300 168 [11] (I refers to interim, and ETS refers to European technical standard). It is designated an interim standard because modifications may be required subsequent to implementation by manufacturers, as the technology is relatively new. In particular, there was no specification for the transmission of data, which has been left to manufacturers to determine. It is possible that a de facto standard will emerge, which could be incorporated into the final ETS. This standard will require faster call setup than the voice system and a modified protocol on the traffic channel. Instead of the usual 4-Kbps signaling for hand shaking, it has been proposed that the full 16-Kbps data rate be used.

The I-ETS has now been through the complete ETSI procedure of public enquiry and formal vote and is available to manufacturers. A second issue containing procedures for the conformance testing of the voice system protocol is about to be published.

Since the original conception of a simple single frequency simplex service, DSRR has expanded into a system that allows two-frequency operation through repeaters and half-duplex operation with base stations. This is because other parts of Europe restrict the licensing of single-frequency operation. A unique feature of DSRR is its ability to allow both single- and two-frequency working to operate side by side without interfering with each other.

CEPT has produced recommendation T/R 75-02, which specifies the operating frequencies and licensing requirements in the CEPT countries. All countries within the European Union have now agreed on the use of these frequencies for DSRR (888–890 MHz paired with 933–935 MHz).

Problems associated with interference to and from DSRR with the GSM services have been perceived, but these have now been largely resolved by the tightening of the blocking specification on DSRR. The control channels have been moved from the band edges to channels 26 and 52, where they should avoid the worst of the splatter caused by GSM. One of the traffic channels has also been deleted to allow for an extra half-channel guard band at the extremes of the frequency allocation. In areas where there may be interference caused by GSM because DSRR uses a free-channel searching protocol, those channels with interference will be avoided and the capacity of DSRR may be reduced locally. Because the maximum output power of a DSRR unit is only 4 watts erp and DSRR is a narrowband FDM signal, it is unlikely that GSM equipment will suffer from interference in the reverse direction, except under very exceptional circumstances. Any interference suffered by GSM equipment will be no worse than—and probably better than—existing interference on normal PMR radio systems, where good site engineering solves the problems of blocking and intermodulation products.

5.5.1 Main Characteristics of DSRR

The DSRR system consists of two control channels and 76 traffic channels operating in the 900-MHz band, with a channel separation of 25 kHz. It is capable of operating in either a single-frequency simplex and/or a two-frequency semi-duplex mode. Direct carrier modulation (GMSK) is used to send the selective signaling codes at 4 Kbps. Voice and data messages are sent at a gross rate of 16 Kbps. The maximum effective radiated power of the transmitter is limited to 4 W. Three principal system elements are specified: units, master units, and repeaters.

The selective signaling code (SSC) consists of a clock synchronization preamble followed by the frame synchronization and a codeword repeated three times.

The speech-coding algorithm for voice transmission and reception is in accordance with the standard adopted within the GSM digital pan-European cellular radio specification. However, the channel coding is different and results in the lower gross bit rate of 16 Kbps.

The coding system used for data transmission and reception is left to the manufacturer's discretion.

5.5.2 Operating Procedure

5.5.2.1 Single-Frequency Working

All radios in the system are normally in the standby state; that is, they are ready to receive a SSC on one of the two control channels. (Units with even serial numbers normally listen on their primary control channel 26 and units with odd serial numbers, on channel 52.) A calling unit first scans and finds a free traffic channel, then communicates via the relevant control channel using the selective signaling code to alert an individual unit or group of units. These units transfer to the traffic channel and enter into conversation. At the end of the conversation, all units return to the standby state.

5.5.2.2 Two-Frequency Working

A similar strategy is adopted with the exception that the protocol is modified so that the master unit or repeater always scans for a free traffic channel irrespective of the origin of the call. Should a two-frequency unit initiate a call, the first SSC contains no traffic channel number (it is set to all zeros) and the master unit or repeater makes the allocation. This is because in most systems of this type, the master station or repeater will have a better antenna position, which gives greater coverage. The master unit or repeater operates in the semi-duplex mode during a conversation (i.e., the transmitter is on permanent transmit) so that any other single- or two-frequency unit is able to recognize that the channel is in use and thus avoid its selection. This is the reason that the single-frequency operating band was chosen to be the same as the base-station transmit band. It also simplified the design of the combined single- and two-frequency unit in that only the transmitter would be required to band switch, leaving the receiver operating in the higher band.

5.5.3 Uses for which DSRR May Be Suitable

One of the great advantages of DSRR is that it has been recognized for use across the European Union without the restrictions usually associated with private mobile radio. It is quite possible for a truck driver to use his unit in the way he now uses his CB (as long as he is aware of other users' SSCs), but he may also obtain local directions for unloading his cargo when arriving at his destination by previous knowledge of the local calling code. Several countries have expressed interest in using DSRR for local communication on farms where either CB or PMR have been previously used. CB has sometimes been inadequate because of local congestion and the open-channel nature of communication, which allows no privacy of conversation, while PMR requires local licensing with its associated costs and bureaucracy. DSRR removes these problems by giving more local capacity with reasonable coverage (approximately a radius of five km from a base or repeater site) and a protocol that inhibits listening in on other conversations. The use of digital modulation also makes it more difficult for a scanner to decode the messages and allows for simple interfacing of data devices for local transfer of messages without the need for speech.

Another possible use that has been identified is where radio equipment is required at a particular location for a temporary purpose, such as road works or sports events. In the past, such incidents have required the issue of a special license or the short-term rental of equipment on special frequencies to give the desired service. These practices may involve undesired extra work for the frequency regulators. DSRR will remove much of this.

There is obviously potential within the standard to develop low-cost, unregulated wireless LAN technology, where other methods may be too expensive because of their reliance on other infrastructure. A DSRR modem could be built into a PC and a corresponding unit in a remote printer, thus allowing greater mobility for the work station. A small office system could easily be developed but, as mentioned earlier, will require some modification to the call setup protocol to improve the speed of access. These modifications could be included in the final ETS, which will be produced in about two years.

In summary, an interim European telecommunications standard has been produced for digital short-range radio. This standard combines the advantages of using multichannel access trunking techniques without requiring a central controller, using digital modulation for voice or data, and the ability to operate in either single- or two-frequency modes. Further, the protocol allows both modes of operation to co-exist with the same frequency allocation in the same geographic area.

References

[1] Cockram, P., and R.H. Tridgell, "An Outline of the Standard Protocol for Band III Trunked Systems," IERE Publication No. 65, *Third International Conference on Land Mobile Radio*, Cambridge, England, December 1985.
[2] Kristiansen, J.A., "Selecting an Optimum Data Format for a Land Mobile Radio Binary Transmission System," *Proc. IEEE 31st Veh. Tech. Conference*, Washington, DC, April 1981, pp. 261–268.

[3]   ETSI, "Technical Characteristics and Test Conditions for Non-Speech and Combined Analogue Speech/Non-Speech Equipment with an Internal and External Antenna Connector, Intended for the Transmission of Data," I-ETS 300 113, Valbonne, France, 1991.

[4]   ETSI, "Binary Interchange of Information and Signaling (BIIS) at 1200 bit/s," I-ETS 300 230, Valbonne, France, 1993.

[5]   ISO 4335, "Information Processing Systems—Data Communications—High Level Data Link Control Element of Procedures," third edition, 1987.

[6]   User Access Definition Group, "Mobile Access Protocol for MPT 1327 Equipment (MAP 27)," version 1.2, UADG, London, August 1993.

[7]   Schoute, P.C. "Control of Aloha Signalling in a Mobile Radio Trunking system," *Proc. IEE Conference on Radio Spectrum Conservation Techniques*, London, July 1980.

[8]   Dewey et al., "Design of the TETRA Mobile Radio Air Interface Protocol," *Proc. IEE Conference on Mobile and Personal Communications*, Brighton, England, December 13–15, 1993.

[9]   CCITT Rec. X.25, 1988.

[10]   Haguenauer, J., "RCPC Codes and their Applications," IEEE COM, April 1988.

[11]   ETSI, "Digital Short Range Radio (DSSR)," I-ETS 300 168, Valbonne, France.

CHAPTER 6

DATA OVER ANALOG AND DIGITAL CELLULAR

Cellular radio networks have been set up primarily for the transmission of mobile voice telephony. They have become regarded as extensions of the fixed public switched telephone network (PSTN). It has become common to use the PSTN as a means of transmission of data by use of modems, which over the years have become capable of higher and higher speeds as the technology has improved both in the modem itself and in the network. The long-awaited advent of the integrated services digital network (ISDN) has not yet happened to any significant degree, so most data transmission still relies on the use of the circuit switched PSTN. Public switched packet data networks (PSPDN) are available and growing, but these networks tend to be used by large business users as extensions or interconnections between private data networks. The architecture of these and the associated cost of the PADs have not yet penetrated the mass user market to any great extent. Similarly, it is difficult to transpose the time-division multiplex (TDM) structure with store-and-forward addressing into the world of cellular radio, where communication is essentially circuit switched. This distinction is becoming blurred with the introduction of digital radio transmission techniques, as used in GSM, which will be discussed later in the chapter.

6.1 DATA OVER AMPS AND TACS ANALOG CELLULAR

The connection of a standard line protocol modem to a cellular phone is possible and has succeeded with varying degrees of success. The bit error rates over the air interface are significantly worse than those encountered on the PSTN, particularly if the vehicle is moving. In addition, the audio path may be muted for significant periods of time by the network and the mobile for the interchange of network control signals, such as handover and power control. These can last for several hundreds of milliseconds. For speech users, this blanking can sometimes be disconcerting but usually passes almost unnoticed. It will cause catastrophic damage to a data stream unless specific precautions are taken.

6.1.1 The Experience in the U.K.

In the U.K., the two cellular operators have adopted different stances to the problem. On behalf of Vodafone, Vodata in conjunction with Racal Research have encouraged the development a specific public domain protocol for data over the air interface. This is known as cellular data link control (CDLC) [1,2], which incorporates both forward error correction (FEC) and automatic repeat request (ARQ) for retransmission of blocks in error that cannot be corrected. This protocol has its roots in HDLC, which includes cyclic redundancy checking (CRC) for the detection of errors.

Cellnet has opted to allow the user to decide which of the available landline standards they would prefer to use and have thus offered transparent working into the PSTN. This is in the belief that as the capacity and coverage of the cellular network improves, so will the quality of the air interface. In addition, it is argued that most data transactions occur when the vehicle is stationary, which reduces the chances of severe loss of data due to fading or burst errors caused by network-control functions.

6.1.2 Cellular Data Link Control Protocol

The CDLC modem modulation is based on the CCITT recommendation V26bis, which allows full-duplex working at 2.4 Kbps in the forward channel and 150 bps in the backward channel. This allows two-wire working and can be useful in maintaining low-cost connections within the network. It is not permissible to use the full-duplex mode on the PSTN in the U.K., as it exceeds the allowed spectral limits of the network. Full-duplex operation from mobile to mobile is possible. Although CDLC-formatted data can be made to traverse the PSTN, this is rarely the case, as it would be necessary to install a corresponding modem at the fixed end. In order to offer as broad a service as possible, Vodafone offers a free data gateway service; the Vodafone Mobile Data Conversion Service (VMACS), which converts the over-air protocol into one of the many standard wireline formats.

Although the gross rate of the forward channel is operating at 2.4 Kbps, the net user rate can drop to approximately half this number due to the application of the FEC and ARQ. The degree of FEC on the forward channel is switched between two levels, depending on the received error rate. In good signal areas, a 72, 68

Reed-Solomon code is used. This switches to a 16, 8 BCH (Bose-Chaudhuri-Hoc-quenghem) code as the error rate increases. If, when the RS code is in use, a retry is requested, the repeat is always sent in BCH. Interleaving of the coded data is used to spread burst errors within a block. This technique greatly increases the ability of the FEC with the type of errors that may be encountered in a mobile radio environment. (see Chapters 3 and 4). The depth of interleaving is variable and is dependent on the length of the transmitted data block. The information about the block length is contained in one of eight synchronization codes. The interleaving depth varies between 1.7 ms to 28.3 ms. Obviously, the greater the depth of interleaving, the longer the burst of errors that can be corrected, but also the longer the delay in the transmission of the data block. A balance has to be struck between these two requirements.

6.1.3 Vodafone Mobile Data Conversion Service (VMACS)

As mentioned earlier, a useful service only becomes a reality if gateways into the available wireline services are provided, because not every user has a CDLC modem at the fixed network end. The VMACS gateway offers connection to the PSTN, the PSPDN, and to private networks. In the case of the PSTN, V21, V22, V22bis, V23, and V42 modem standards can be supported [2].

The mobile user does not need to know which of the above standards is implemented as the gateway adapts itself to the called modem's data rate and modulation. The data rate of the CDLC modem and the wireline modem may be different, but this is catered for by flow control utilizing the clear-to-send (CTS) function. The procedure for access is to dial 972 followed by the full telephone number of the called party, including the area code.

Calls in the opposite direction, from PSTN users to mobiles, are set-up using two-stage over dialing. First the VMACS gateway is contacted using a normal area code and telephone number, and when the call is established, the mobile number is dialed (without the cellular access area code) using DTMF signaling.

Access to the PSPDN is gained by use of a packet assembler/disassembler (PAD), which is permanently connected into the fixed network. To gain access to this service, not only is it necessary for the mobile to access the gateway (by dialing 970 followed by the particular network's three digit access code), it is also necessary to use a password and conventional log-on procedures.

The private networks are accessed by dialing 973 followed by the particular network's identity. Connection is by digital multiplexers connected to 64-Kbps channels on the Vodanet private network. Vodanet users may easily make calls in the reverse direction.

6.2 CELLULAR DIGITAL PACKET DATA

In the U.S., data have been transmitted across the circuit-switched network in a similar fashion to the methods used in the U.K. However, there have been two initiatives for a genuine packet data service overlaid on the cellular infrastructure, one of which appears to be faltering and the other gathering momentum. The method that appears to be losing favor is called CDI and will only be discussed briefly.

The architecture of this system is based on the observation that there is unused spectrum situated between the 30-kHz separated carriers in the AMPS cellular structure. In addition, adjacent channels are not normally used within the same cell or sector, which allows more tolerance in adjacent channel performance. It has been proposed that this *spare* spectrum could support an *interstitial carrier* upon which a time-division multiplexed (TDM) packet data modulation could be superimposed. This carrier could carry data at a gross rate of between 2.4 and 4.8 Kbps without causing any degradation to the cellular network. The argument for doing this is that the incremental cost of equipping existing cellular sites would be small because the fixed network communications links would be in place and the additional base stations would be relatively inexpensive. The cost of the mobiles may be significant, as they are unlikely to be integrated within the normal cellular handset.

The other proposal, which has gained significant support from the computer industry and several of the U.S. cellular operators, including IBM, GTE, McCaw, and Pactel, is known as CDPD and is at a much more advanced stage. A preliminary release of the specification has been made [3] and trials have been conducted in the San Francisco Bay Area. Unlike CDI, it is intended that CDPD shares the cellular channel frequencies but does not use the same base-station infrastructure. It is proposed that the data packets are sent during periods of low activity on the voice network, even to the extent of using the call setup time of a voice call to transmit short status-type messages. (It is unlikely that the latter will be attempted in the early stages, as the complexity of control is very high). This allows the full bandwidth of the 30-kHz separated channel to be used and thus allows a gross data rate of 19.2 Kbps, using GMSK modulation without exceeding the limits of adjacent channel performance.

6.2.1 CDPD Network Architecture

The CDPD network is restricted in its scope by the regional nature of cellular voice networks and, as a result, has to operate in a similar way to a service-provider network. Within a service provider's region, the following interfaces come under the provider's control:

- The air interface;
- The interservice provider interface (between service providers);
- The external interface (between the CDPD network and other fixed networks)

6.2.2 CDPD Air Interface

The air interface operates between the mobile data base station (MDBS) and the mobile-end system (M-ES). Its characteristics are listed in Table 6.1:

TABLE 6.1
The Characteristics of the CDPD Air Interface

Mobile Tx frequency	824–849 MHz
Mobile Rx frequency	869–894 MHz
Channel separation	30 kHz
Modulation	Gaussian minimum shift keyed
Bit rate	19.2 Kbps
Mobile Tx power	0.6, 1.6, and 4 watts
Packet protocol	TCP/IP
DTE interface	AT-compatible

The media access control (MAC) layer protocol has been specifically designed for CDPD and uses a slotted digital sense multiple access with collision detection (DSMA/CD) protocol on the access channel. This access channel can also be the main traffic channel under light-load conditions. A rate (63, 39) Reed-Solomon code is used for error correction on blocks of 378 bits. Four of these blocks are concatenated to form a maximum user packet size of 116 bytes. If additional network synchronization and management overhead—for example, of 10%—is added, the net data rate equates to approximately 10.5 Kbps, which would allow for a level of ARQ if a standard user rate of 9.6 Kbps is to be attempted.

6.2.3 Network Layer

The network layer reference diagram is shown in Figure 6.1. There are three basic infrastructure elements in CDPD.

1. The MDBS provides a data link relay and is not strictly a network layer entity.
2. The mobile data intermediate system (MD-IS) is the only network element that stores the registration and the location of a mobile unit. There are two logical functions associated with the MD-IS. First, every mobile has a home function MD-IS and all calls to a mobile are routed via this element. If the mobile has roamed, the call is rerouted to the other MD-IS on which the mobile has registered as a visiting unit. This second function is known as the mobile service function.
3. The intermediate system is a traffic router, which uses standard wireline protocols that support TCP/IP or OSI 8473. This element and its associated physical interconnections are the CDPD network backbone.

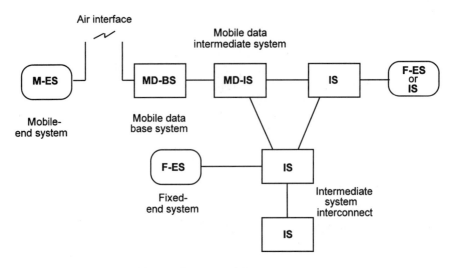

FIGURE 6.1 CDPD network layer reference model.

The over-air protocol has to be converted into a network-layer protocol at the MD-IS.

6.3 DATA OVER GSM DIGITAL CELLULAR

The global system for mobile communications (GSM)—which was once called Groupe Spécial Mobile but was renamed when it became clear that the market extended outside Europe—is inherently a digital system with architectural roots in ISDN. The main difference between these technologies with respect to the transparent transmission of data are the different data rates of the internal carriers. ISDN operates with a basic rate of 64 Kbps, and the GSM channel has a gross full channel rate of only 22.8 Kbps. Due to the hostile nature of the radio channel, this includes significant channel coding. By the use of data-rate converters, it is possible to obtain a user data rate of 9.6 Kbps on a full-rate channel and rate of 4.8 Kbps on a half-rate channel. Obviously, with various coding rates and interleaving distances, it is possible to offer slower rates than these.

The basic GSM radio carrier operates at a data rate of 270 Kbps (270.833 Kbps to be more exact) using 0.3 BT GMSK modulation. The channel separation between the carriers is 200 kHz, but because of the high level of adjacent channel power, it is not possible for contiguous carriers to operate from the same site. Each carrier is divided into time slots enabling eight full-rate channels to be supported. Additional overhead for signaling and control purposes is also included. The slot structure is designed so that it is possible to split the eight full-rate channels by a factor of two. When the half-rate codec is finally agreed, the system will be able to support 16 half-rate channels. The same slot structure is maintained for the trans-

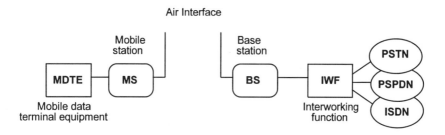

FIGURE 6.2 Data transfer schematic.

mission of voice and data, and thus a variable mix is possible on a single carrier simultaneously.

Unlike transmission over an analog network, it is not necessary to use modems. However, it is necessary to incorporate data gateways so that conversion to other network protocols (PSTN, ISDN, PSPDN, etc.) can be accomplished. These gateways are known collectively as the interworking function (IWF). A typical example of data-rate conversion within GSM is as follows:

Mobile data terminal rate	9.6 Kbps
Converted in the mobile to	12.0 Kbps
Transmitted at	22.8 Kbps (includes channel coding and FEC)
Converted at the Base station to	16 or 64 Kbps ISDN rate
Converted at the IWF to	9.6 Kbps line modem connection to the PSTN.

The data-rate adapter in the mobile is based on the CCITT V110-rate adapters used in ISDN [4] but with some modification to satisfy the particular needs of the GSM. In particular, a new version of RA1 called RA1' has been developed to satisfy the internal interface data rates of 3.6, 6.0, and 12 Kbps, as required by the GSM standard [5].

6.3.1 Transparent and Nontransparent Working

The transmission of data over different networks can be characterized by different forms of working, which can sometimes seem ambiguous. The terms *connection-oriented* and *connectionless data* are often confused with the similar terms *transparent* and *nontransparent working*. It is worthwhile spending a little time making sure that the true meanings are fully understood.

Connection-oriented operation is when a complete circuit is established from end to end before any transaction takes place. This could be the case of a telephone call, where the circuit, which is likely to be a mixture of copper wire, fiber-optic cable, microwave, mobile radio, and perhaps a satellite link, is established before an essentially real-time interchange of information can occur. This means that all the links in the chain must be available simultaneously. This, therefore, does not make best use of the available resources, as additional equipment is necessary to meet the peak traffic load, which may vary at different times and at different points in the network. Also, time is lost at certain parts of the network as the link is established. On the other hand, in a connectionless environment, only the link between nodes need be established for the traffic to pass. The data is stored at each node until connection is possible to the next point along the route. By time-sharing of resources in this way, much greater efficiency of use of the communications links can be achieved. This method of working is unsuitable for speech but is quite acceptable for most data transfers. This often referred to as *store and forward*.

Transparent operation is the transfer of traffic without the involvement of the network in verifying the accuracy of the data transferred. For instance, data could be encoded in an application to traverse a network and contain error-detection codes, which could be invoked to ascertain whether the received data is correct or not. Because of the hostile nature of the radio channel, it may be that the network uses an error-correction code with interleaving but does not check for resultant errors. The data will arrive at its destination and may contain some errors, but it is up to the application to decide what should be done about them. This is particularly important with respect to the transmission of digital speech, which has to be received in real time. In nontransparent operation, in addition to providing the FEC and interleaving, the network also provides error checking of the data packets. Should a packet arrive with errors that cannot be corrected, a request for the packet to be resent (ARQ) is made. The data will not be forwarded until correct packets are available, unless the transmission path has failed, in which case no data will be forwarded. A suitable algorithm decides on the optimum number of retry attempts to be invoked before giving up. This means that a variable delay may be introduced over the data path. In transparent operation, the end application is able to make this request if required. However, in a connectionless environment, it is preferable for the network to make the ARQs over each link in the chain, thus ensuring that data integrity is maintained over the whole path.

In summary, transparent operation tends to be associated with the connection-oriented environment and nontransparent, with the connectionless environment, but this is not always the case. GSM offers both transparent and nontransparent services in an essentially connection-oriented network. In the future, it is expected that connectionless services will be offered but the relevant specifications for the infrastructure have yet to be produced.

6.3.2 GSM Transparent Service

The transparent service is capable of supporting both synchronous and asynchronous data terminals. As explained above, the service does not guarantee data integrity, but it offers a typical level of residual bit error rate due to the overall nature of the GSM system. For instance, if the channel gross bit error rate becomes too bad, then either the circuit breaks down or, more likely, a handover will occur to switch the user to a better channel. Due to the basic TDM structure of GSM and the need for channel coding and interleaving, a fixed delay of about 100 ms occurs end to end in the system (GSM 04.xx series). Note that the end-to-end speech delay using the full-rate codec is aimed at being less than 40 ms. At 9.6 Kbps in a full-rate channel, the typical residual bit error rate is of the order of 1 in 10^{-3}. At 4.8 Kbps, this improves to about 1 in 10^{-4} and at slower rates, it is better than 1 in 10^{-5}.

6.3.3 Rate Adaptation

In ISDN the RA1 adapter standard converts the 9.6-Kbps data from the terminal equipment into 16 Kbps for transmission over the network. This is achieved by sampling the incoming data into 5-ms frames (48 data bits) and packing the frames with an additional 32 bits to become a total of 80 bits. The packing is in accordance with the V110 standard [4]. The additional bits comprise of frame and byte synchronization bits as well as one complete byte (the E bits), which contains the original data-rate information.

The modified RA1' adapter for use on GSM packs the data out to a 60-bit frame by adding a further 12 bits. This is because there is synchronization operational in the TDM structure and also the data-rate information is sent over a separate control channel. The data are then clocked into the forward error corrector at 12 Kbps. An example of the conversion timing is shown in Figure 6.3 below.

For conversion from 4.8 Kbps to 6 Kbps, the same structure is maintained by increasing the sampling period to 10 ms. For lower data rates, a different frame size is used, and 24 data bits are converted into 36 bit frames [5].

6.3.4 GSM Nontransparent Service

The nontransparent service uses a radio-link protocol (RLP) [6], which has been derived from HDLC (ISO 4335). To maintain a user rate of at least 9.6 Kbps over the radio path, the RLP takes four of the RA1' 60-bit frames and inputs them to the forward error corrector at 12 Kbps. Instead of the normal 16-bit frame check sum (FCS), a 24 bit FCS is used to combat the expected high bit error rate. The FEC part operates with a modulus of 64 to minimize the round-trip delay. In addition, it allows 10% of the channel capacity to be reserved for ARQs without compromising the 9.6-Kbps true user rate on a full-rate channel. This typically enables true user

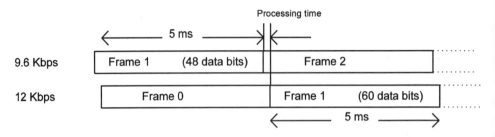

FIGURE 6.3 RA1' frame structure.

rate operation over 90% of a cell area for 90% of the time. At other times, circuit 105 and 106 control will have to be invoked at the terminal equipment.

The transmission of RLP frames is synchronized with the TDM frame structure of the GSM network, and all addressing is carried by that network, thus removing this overhead from the link protocol.

6.3.5 Short Message Service and Cell Broadcast

Two very important network services using data transfer are incorporated in GSM. The short message service (SMS) [7,8] allows data to be transferred between mobiles and a message service center. The service center is connected via several gateways to other service providers, which could include a paging service, a news service, or a road information service. Messages are limited to 160 characters and can be bidirectional. Messages to a mobile may be either displayed on the mobile itself, if it has a suitable display, or on a terminal device connected to it. Similarly, messages can be sent from the mobile's keypad or from the terminal device.

The SMS service center is configured to store messages that cannot be delivered when the mobile is out of range or switched off and forward them when the network indicates that it has become available. Two forms of message transfer are specified: an individual message, which is sent to a specific mobile, and a broadcast message, which can be received by subscribers to the service within a particular cell. Road traffic and weather information are ideally suited to this form of information dissemination.

The short message data are transferred across the radio interface simultaneously with signaling messages. The two data flows are distinguished from each other by a link identifier called the service access point identifier (SAPI). The use of the term SAPI was inherited from ISDN and is not the correct use of OSI terminology where data link connection identifier (DLCI) is used in this context. SAPI 0 identifies the signaling part and SAPI 3, the SMS part. The data flow occurs on the TCH/8 logical channel and allows data transfer at the equivalent of approximately 600 bps over the air interface [9].

6.4 CONCLUSIONS

Circuit-connected data facilities have been available on the cellular networks from the very early days, even if it was only the use of landline protocol modems connected at the end points. A user need for data has been present but, partly due to the costs involved and lack of suitable equipment, has never become a significant part of the network traffic. With the advent of the latest digital networks and the increasing awareness of the consumer, data transmission is set to follow the explosive growth of the speech traffic on the cellular networks across the world. It is expected that data on the predominantly speech-oriented cellular telephone networks will be complementary to the dedicated public mobile data networks, and each will find particular applications that offer the most cost-effective solutions. The CDPD system may be regarded as a hybrid, as it offers packet-data connection similar to that of the dedicated networks but uses part of the cellular infrastructure and frequency resource. In a similar vein, the introduction of true packet services on the GSM will also begin to blur the differences between the functions of the various current systems. Ultimately, with the advent of UMTS, it is expected that ubiquitous personal telecommunications services will become available to all mobile users.

References

[1] Frazer, E.L., I. Harris, and P. Munday, "CDLC—A Data Transmission Standard for Cellular Radio," *Journal of the IERE,* Vol. 57, No 3, May/June 1987, pp. 129–133.

[2] Davie, M.C., and J.B. Smith, "A Cellular Packet Radio Network," *Electronics and Communications Engineering Journal* (IEE), Vol. 3, No. 3, June 1991, pp. 137–143.

[3] McCaw Cellular et al., CDPD System Specifications, Preliminary Release 0.8, March 1993.

[4] V110, "Support of Data Terminal Equipment with V Series Type Interfaces by an Integrated Services Digital Network," Geneva, September 1992.

[5] ETSI, "Rate Adaptation at the MS BSS Interface," GSM Recommendation 04.21, Valbonne, France

[6] ETSI, "Radio Link Protocol," GSM Recommendation 04.22, Valbonne, France.

[7] ETSI, "Short Message Service (SMS)," GSM Recommendation 03. 40, Valbonne, France.

[8] ETSI, "SMS Cell Broadcast," GSM Recommendation 03. 41, Valbonne, France.

[9] Mouly, M., M.-B. Pautet, *The GSM System for Mobile Communications,* Paris, France, 1992.

CHAPTER 7
▼▼▼

MOBILE DATA NETWORKS

Over the last few years, as radio channels have become more difficult to obtain, data communications have become more important in the mobile radio environment. Simulations and practice have shown that some 20 to 25 users may be supported on one duplex cellular radio channel, around 100 on a half-duplex dispatcher system, and about 600 on a data system for similar grades of service. Obviously, the usage is quite different, but it has also been shown that many telephone calls could easily be replaced by a data call, in some cases with greater reliability, as the recipient may end up with a hard copy for later reference. It is no wonder that the radio regulators, who have the day-to-day headache of allocating radio frequencies to would-be users, have been enthusiastic about licensing data networks. In the U.K. and on continental Europe, data networks are now being licensed in increasing numbers. Until the advent of the TETRA standard (see Chapter 5), there has been no pan-European standard, and the following proprietary systems have emerged.

7.1 PAKNET

The Paknet system was originally designed for fixed point-to-point radio data communication as an alternative to copper-wire telecommunication. Subsequently, as a result of competition from the mobile data networks, they were awarded an extension to their license and allowed to include mobile units.

The protocol has been optimized for the transmission of *bursty* data packets of around 1,000 bits [1]. The reason for this is that packets of data in excess of this may be better transported by other means, such as circuit-switched connection over the PSTN or by data over cellular. Another solution is to use the PSPDN, but this requires a large number of remote terminals to be concentrated at a given location to be economic and justify the cost of a trunk. The initial market identified was the *electronic funds transfer from the point of sale* (EFTPOS) business, where credit card validation is required very quickly, usually less than 10 seconds, and at an economic cost. This can be achieved by means of a telephone connection, and very often is, but the time and cost of making the call can be prohibitive. Another advantage of the radio solution is that store layouts may be altered without the need to involve the telephone company in installing new access points. In larger stores this may be achieved by the use of a wireless LAN operating into a fixed access point, which itself is connected either into the telephone network or to the wireless data network. Semimobile point-of-sale units may be deployed easily at trade shows, sporting events, etc., without the need for a copper connection.

Other uses for which this particular protocol is suited include remote telemetry, security alarm monitoring and signaling, and simple forms of two-way messaging. Paknet has been successful in the traffic-monitoring field, whether just counting traffic or supplying the means of transporting road congestion data for the Traffic Master system. Traffic Master sensors mounted on highway bridges use the packet radio service to relay information on traffic movement back to a control center. Details of concentrated traffic spots are then broadcast to special display units mounted in subscribers' vehicles to allow drivers to reroute and avoid the traffic jams. The utility companies have expressed interest for remote meter reading and monitoring of their remote unmanned installations. In the security field, a radio alarm can sometimes be a very useful backup if there is a possibility of the telephone wires being cut. It is also very useful when a temporary installation is required, as there is no need to set up leased lines for the purpose.

7.1.1   Access Protocol

A derivative of slotted aloha [2] was specially developed and is known as dynamic slotted reservation aloha (DSRA). It is claimed that this technique, although it has greater control overhead than pure random-access techniques, gives greater throughput for mixtures of long and short data packets. Simulation had shown that fixed-assignment techniques such as TDMA are efficient when the number of terminals is small and the traffic load is predictable. Random techniques such as slotted aloha and carrier sense multiple access (CSMA) are more efficient when the number of terminals is large and the packet sizes are small. DSRA is a compromise between these methods.

The channels are divided into time slots of approximately 27 ms duration. All remote units gain system synchronization by monitoring the downlink channel. Control messages on the downlink define uplink slots that may be used for random access, and if a terminal unit has data to send it will randomly pick one of these slots and make a request. Contained in the request telegram is information about the size of packet awaiting transmission, so the controller is able to acknowledge the request with an allocation of the correct number of slots. Figure 7.1 depicts a Packnet slot.

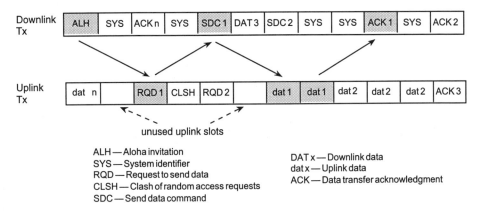

FIGURE 7.1 Paknet slot diagram.

The number of slots allocated for random access can be varied depending on the traffic statistics as viewed by the controller. For example, if it is noted that there are a large number of short messages being received from many different terminals, then a larger number of random-access slots must be offered to avoid multiple collisions. Conversely, if the messages are long packets, greater efficiency is obtained by the reduction of the number of random-access slots.

7.1.2 Air Interface

As mentioned in Section 7.1.1, each frame is approximately 27 ms long, and the data is transmitted at 8 Kbps using narrow shift binary frequency shift keying (FSK). This is a very simple means of transmission, which requires minimal pre-modulation filtering. It is not as robust as GMSK but, on economic grounds, was found to be adequate for relatively simple, low-cost radio units. The radio network is planned using cellular techniques. The channel frequencies are planned from a contiguous block and adjacent channels are not used at the same site, which means that it is possible to operate at slightly greater than normal adjacent channel power in a 12.5-kHz allocation without causing interference to other mobile radio users.

7.1.3 Error Protection

Each frame has a 12-bit cyclic redundancy checksum added to it before it is encoded with a forward error correction (FEC) code. All data within the frame are encoded using a Golay code (see Chapter 4). This allows the correction of up to any three errors in a 24-bit block. If the CRC detects any residual errors impossible to correct, the protocol initiates an ARQ on the blocks in error and requests their selective retransmission.

7.1.4 Network Addresses

The Paknet system has an addressing scheme that is compatible with CCITT X.121, where each entity is assigned a 14-digit address. Each base site is defined by eight of the digits, and the remaining six define a unique terminal. The Paknet network has been allocated its own international number (DNIC) in accordance with the CCITT X.121 recommendation. This allows direct interconnection to other public data networks using X.75 interconnections. International access can be established via the Mercury public data network service (MDNS).

The radio network is capable of transmitting broadcast messages to a group of radio terminal units that have been allocated a second address.

7.1.5 Terminal Interfaces

At the subscriber radio unit, an asynchronous interface in accordance with V24/28, RS 232 signaling is available. For call control, three possible signaling options are offered, which can be selected by the end user. First an X.28 standard asynchronous access to an X.25 PAD simulates what is available on a fixed network. Most of the control signaling is carried out on the transmit-and-receive data lines.

Second, an implementation that simulates V25bis procedures to a standard modem is available, which allows for the use of hard-wire connections for control purposes. Finally, there is an asynchronous TPAD mode, which is commonly used in the EFTPOS mode of working.

7.1.6 System Architecture

The radio network is built up on a seven-cell frequency reuse pattern, which is suitable for the level of cochannel interference that can be tolerated. Each radio channel at a base station has its own dedicated line back to the X.25 packet switch exchange. This allows some redundancy in the network, as there are always at least two radio units at each base site. Should one of the channels at a site fail, a subscriber unit will always retune automatically to the other channel. Should a complete base station fail, the subscriber unit is capable of retuning to another base site if there is sufficient RF coverage.

Fixed-point land line users are connected into the network via PADs on the X.25 network, which is part of the Mercury fixed telecommunications network (MDNS). Radio unit to radio unit calls are routed via the switching centers irrespective of their location. Unlike Mobitex, there is no hierarchical structure to minimize network involvement should units be located near the same base site (see Section 7.2).

The system was originally designed as a fixed radio network but, as mentioned earlier, has been given a license extension to allow mobile operation. To date, the customer base is still predominantly made up of fixed users, but additions to the protocol have been made to allow limited roaming from their *home* sites. The other networks described in this chapter were all designed for mobile operation from the outset.

7.2 MOBITEX

Mobitex uses a different access method, which is a modified form of carrier sense multiple access (CSMA). A similar technique is used on the AMPS/TACS cellular control channel—the busy/idle bit in the overhead message. The base station periodically transmits an (SVP) signal (known as a *sweep* message), which contains network identification and network parameter information. For instance, the signal (SVP1) contains mobile roaming parameters and another signal (SVP6) contains similar information for handportable equipment, which operates at lower power. If a mobile wishes to send a message to the system, it must wait until it has received a (SVP) and a *free signal* (FRI) message, which indicates that a certain number of following slots are available for random access. Each mobile that has a message to send, internally generates a random-access number, which determines the time at which it will attempt access after detection of the (FRI) signal. The mobile with the lowest number gains access and the network generates an acknowledgment that stops the other units from attempting access until a new (FRI) signal is detected. Should two subscriber units generate the same number and transmit at the same time and cause corruption, no acknowledgment will be forthcoming, so a mobile with a higher access number will attempt access in its later time slot. An exception to this rule is the case of a mobile that becomes ready to send a message during a (FRI) frame. This mobile is allowed to attempt access in the very next slot.

Unlike reservation aloha, the protocol does not require the base station to tell the mobile when it may send its main message. Messages up to 512 octets may be sent immediately if the network parameters allow it. If the base station recognizes that long messages are being sent, it will transmit a SILENCE signal to all other mobiles, which tells them they may not transmit. This command is only canceled by receipt of a new (FRI) signal.

The access algorithm parameters may be changed dynamically by the network operator depending on the traffic situation. The maximum size of the message and the levels of traffic priority may be altered. In addition, the number of random slots from which the mobiles may choose can be altered as the traffic density changes. (The number of slots must be increased as the traffic load increases to reduce the probability of contention.) The length of the free slots can be changed to accommodate typical message lengths and the maximum access parameter can be changed to prevent messages longer than a free slot from being sent. Under these circumstances, the SILENCE signal is not required. If a long message must be sent, it can either be split up into shorter messages at the mobile or a long message request can be made, which may cause the network to allocate an alternative traffic channel or invoke the SILENCE parameter.

7.2.1 Message Format

The over-air message format is made up of frame head, primary blocks, and following blocks, as shown in Figure 7.2.

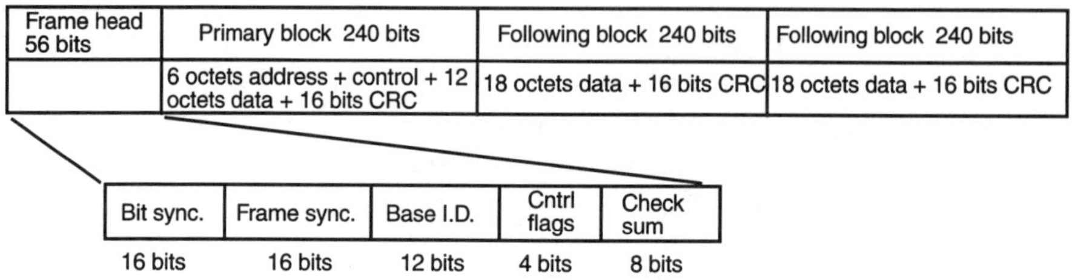

Frame head 56 bits	Primary block 240 bits	Following block 240 bits	Following block 240 bits
	6 octets address + control + 12 octets data + 16 bits CRC	18 octets data + 16 bits CRC	18 octets data + 16 bits CRC

Bit sync.	Frame sync.	Base I.D.	Cntrl flags	Check sum
16 bits	16 bits	12 bits	4 bits	8 bits

FIGURE 7.2 MOBITEX radio frame.

The data to be transmitted is first assembled into Mobitex packets (MPAK), which consist of 144 data bits (this includes the address and control bits in the case of the primary packet) to which are appended 16 cyclic redundancy-check bits in accordance with CRC-CCITT X.25.

It should be noted that in the primary and following blocks, there is a discrepancy between the number of bits of data and CRC (160 bits) and the number of bits actually transmitted (240 bits). This is because additional error correction in the form of a shortened (12,8) Hamming coding is added. This allows at least one error per block to be successfully corrected. Also, interleaving to a depth of 20 is used within a block, which means that it is theoretically possible to correct burst errors up to 20 bits long. Only complete blocks may be sent because of the requirement of the block interleaving, so if the last block is incomplete, the remaining part of the MPAK is filled with all zeros. The frame header is not coded and the full falsing protection afforded by the CRC is maintained. A burst error of 16 bits in length within the MPAK would be required to give false detection. This is extremely unlikely, particularly with the use of interleaving.

However, there is another feature that may be used with bidirectional transmission, the automatic repeat request (ARQ) protocol. If a data packet, even after correction, still contains errors, a request can be sent for it to be repeated. Mobitex contains this facility in the form of selective ARQ, which means that only the block in error, not the whole message, need be repeated.

7.2.2 System Architecture

A typical medium-sized system is shown in Figure 7.3. A notable feature of the Mobitex architecture is that because sufficient intelligence is built into each node, messages have to travel up the hierarchy only as high as a common node. For example, if a call from mobile to mobile can be set up on one base station, the call involves no other part of the network except call-log information, which is sent up to the NCC for billing purposes.

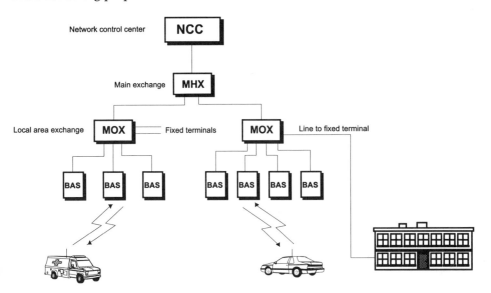

FIGURE 7.3 Mobitex system architecture.

Most fixed terminals are connected to local area exchanges (MOX) by means of land lines, but it is possible to connect directly at a base station if this is economic. Fixed terminals may also be connected to main exchanges (MHX), but this is less usual. In most cases, MHXs and MOXs share a location to save on building rentals.

Connection in the U.K. between main nodes is accomplished by means of *kilostream* circuits operating at 64 Kbps and rented from British Telecom. This includes connection to the base stations. The line network is continuously monitored by network-control equipment and allows the operator at the NCC to "see" the control panels of remote units. (A computer simulation of the distant control panel is presented to the operator on a workstation). Should a line become faulty, it is a very simple task to set up alternative routing.

The MOXs and MHXs share the same hardware and differ only by means of function and software personality. Gateways to the MOX include connection to remote terminals, PSPDN, PABX, and PSTN, as well as connections to base stations, other MOXs, and MHXs. The architecture is modular so it is quite possible to put together a small system with no MHXs or a large international system with multiple MHXs at several levels of hierarchy together with duplicate NCCs. The address field for the subscriber numbers contains 24 bits, which allows for international roaming.

7.2.3 Roaming

When designing mobile data systems for wide-area coverage, it is necessary to incorporate algorithms to allow the subscriber units to migrate from one base station to another. In the case of paging it must be assumed that a receiver can be anywhere on the system, and the paging call must be sent to all base stations for transmission. This results in a net reduction in spectrum efficiency from what could be achieved if the approximate location of the pager is known. Packet data systems exhibit advantages over both paging systems and cellular radio when it comes to roaming. In the case of cellular there is a requirement to *hand over* in real time; otherwise, the speech call will be interrupted. This requirement gives rise to very complex monitoring of each call in progress. Dropped calls have been the biggest source of complaint to the cellular operators, and extra equipment had to be installed to remedy the problem.

Packet data does not require a continuous-circuit connection, as the content of a packet is stored at each node prior to onward transmission. For example, if a mobile does not receive an acknowledgment of a packet because it has just left the coverage area of a particular base station, it will search for another in its neighbor list, determine that it is suitable, and then repeat the packet. As the packet has a unique address and identity, it will be delivered to the correct location and be assembled in the correct order. The network then updates its location register for that mobile so that outgoing messages may be correctly routed. Unlike cellular, the roaming is controlled by the mobile, not by the network, which reduces the network's complexity.

However, it does shift the burden to the mobile, which becomes more complex in that it becomes necessary for it to measure received signal strength and data error rates with some degree of accuracy. It also must keep an up-to-date register of adjacent base sites, together with their signal strengths, and calculate the optimum point at which a change of channel is needed. Changing too often will put an unnecessary burden of reregistrations on the network and changing too little may result in the unit being out of contact for periods of time. A further complication is that mobiles and portables require slightly different criteria when determining a channel change. This criteria also vary according to the environment, e.g., urban, inside or outside of buildings, suburban, or rural. As mentioned earlier, Mobitex caters for this by issuing different (SVP) signals to vary the personality of the subscriber unit according to its location.

7.2.4 Mailbox Facility

A unique feature of packet data systems is the ability to *store and forward* data packets. This means that if in any part of the network a connection cannot be made, the data is stored until such connection is possible. This allows the possibility of sending packets even though it is known that the recipient is unavailable. For instance, a service company such as a gas utility could download the nonurgent installation jobs for its fitters the previous evening. These would then be sent automatically to the mobiles at switch-on the following morning. Mobitex contains this feature, but to make sure the system memory does not become overloaded with excessive rubbish, it only holds messages for, say, 24 hours before deleting them. The time is network programmable and may be longer or shorter depending on the available storage. Unless the mailbox facility is specifically invoked, normal messages are allowed a reasonable time for delivery before they, too, are erased. The sender of the message can be advised that the message was not delivered.

7.2.5 Mobitex Air Interface

Data are encoded into MPAKS and then further channel encoded as shown in Figure 7.2. The smallest message is a status call, which consists of the frame head and primary block only. The maximum message size that may be sent for any access is limited to 512 octets of user data, which equates to 30 data blocks with simple addressing or 31 data blocks with extended addressing. The time taken for the transmission of the minimum telegram is 37 ms at an over air rate of 8 Kbps using GMSK modulation with a BT value of 0.3. This signal is constrained within a 12.5-kHz separated channel. The maximum-length message without extended addressing and assuming no retries takes 907 ms to travel across the air interface. For a message of maximum length, the net data rate to the end user can be equated from:

$$
\begin{aligned}
\text{Total number of packets} &= 30 \\
\text{Number of octets} &= 512 \\
\text{Time taken} &= 907 \text{ ms} \\
\text{Therefore effective data rate} &= 512 \times {}^8/_{0.907} \text{ bps} \\
&\cong 4.6 \text{ Kbps}
\end{aligned}
$$

However, in packet data systems the quality measure should not be the data rate, as that can vary from node to node with the slowest very often being the air interface. The measurement should be the response time across the network, which depends more on the traffic loading and the architecture. The effects of traffic load can be altered by varying the quantity of equipment installed, which leaves the network architecture as the main factor in the assessment of network quality.

7.3 COGNITO

Cognito uses a basic TDMA method for multiple access that adheres to a much more rigid structure than either of the previous two systems discussed. As mentioned in Section 7.1.1, simulations have shown that the TDMA method is very efficient for the transfer of regular-sized packets from a relatively small number of users, but becomes less so if it is necessary to cope with a high level of diverse traffic with variable message lengths. The market that has been initially been identified has been the *white goods* service area, where technicians visit domestic premises, transmit back to base fixed-length report forms, and receive preformatted instructions. This application has been working alongside the Messager service, which may be likened to acknowledgment paging with very short messages. This mix has proved to be successful in the marketplace.

7.3.1 Access Protocol

Slotted aloha is used as the basic mechanism for random access to the network [3]. A 12-slot, network configurable frame is usually used with two quarter uplink slots per frame made available for mobile units to gain access to the system, and a further two quarter slots made available for registration. The frame length may be adjusted between 10 and 18 slots per frame at the time of site installation and depends on the predicted traffic pattern. Each slot lasts for 125 ms, which is equivalent to 768 bits at the over-air rate of 6.144 Kbps. The downlink path is able to make use of this full capacity, but guard times of 36 bits are included in the uplink path to allow for timing errors and propagation delays.

Slots in each frame are reserved for particular system subservices, with the first slot of the frame always reserved for general control. This is to provide a mobile unit with information that enables it to register on the system at that particular base station. The capacity of a single slot is not usually sufficient to carry all of the data that the mobile needs, so different data are carried on the first slot of subsequent frames until a complete cycle of frames has been transmitted. The cycle is then repeated. A mobile is required to gather all of this information before it is allowed to make a registration attempt.

One slot, slot two in the example, is reserved for the *down setup*. This is to tell a mobile unit that there is a call waiting and that it will be transmitted in specified following slots. The fixed nature of this setup slot in the TDMA structure allows a simple method of implementing battery saving in the portable units. The receivers of portables and mobiles need only be active during this particular slot, which allows an immediate duty cycle saving of the order of 10:1. Further savings can be accomplished by operating in the very low duty cycle (VLDC) mode, where the network has been informed that the portable wishes to operate in this way and then only has a paging opportunity once every cycle of frames (each multiframe). This gives significantly improved battery life but messages can be delayed. This feature is user-selectable. Similar techniques are used in paging networks, in particular in the European radio message system (ERMES)[4]. This system is very sophisticated and supports pan-European roaming. It is time-locked to UTC; it has multiple framing levels, which allow different battery saving algorithms; and it operates on 16 channels, which have been reserved across most countries of the European Union and many CEPT-member countries. (Concern has been expressed about the frequencies allocated, as it has been shown that interference is possible with low-specification television receivers operating in Band III due to mixing with the image of the sound subcarrier.)

Other slots have fixed allocations for registration, data transfer, and acknowledgments, as shown in Figure 7.4. Data transfers may be allocated by the base station for transmission in subsequent slots. Before the mobile registers, it is given information about the particular base station with which it is working, such as the slots it may use to register, the mobile group label (MGL), which must be used to register, the base station *color code* and identity, and the frequencies of neighboring cells. The color code is an identifier that determines the difference between stations operating on the same frequency, so that unwanted cochannel signals may be ignored. This technique is used in both the AMPS and TACS cellular systems, where different out-of-band analog tones are used as color codes.

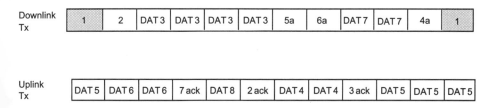

Downlink Tx

| 1 | 2 | DAT 3 | DAT 3 | DAT 3 | DAT 3 | 5a | 6a | DAT 7 | DAT 7 | 4a | 1 |

Uplink Tx

| DAT 5 | DAT 6 | DAT 6 | 7 ack | DAT 8 | 2 ack | DAT 4 | DAT 4 | 3 ack | DAT 5 | DAT 5 | DAT 5 |

1. First slot for general control.
2. Down setup.
3. DAT 3 Base to mobile data transfer.
4. Note that DAT 5 from mobile to base carries over from one frame to the next.

FIGURE 7.4 Cognito frame structure.

7.3.2 Air Interface

The gross data rate is 6.144 Kbps, and Cognito uses Gaussian filtered frequency shift keyed (GFSK) modulation on carriers in the 175-MHz part of the spectrum [3]. The data rate is slightly lower than that used by either Paknet or Mobitex to support low-cost radios and to meet the full regulatory requirement for adjacent channel power with no compromise. This is because the frequency allocations are interspersed between other public access mobile radio (PAMR) users. A feature of the modulation scheme is that a coded sequence is superimposed on the data stream before transmission to minimize the direct current (dc) component in the modulation. The primary objective of this is to allow the use of single-point excited phase lock loop synthesizers in the transmitters and avoid dc coupling in the receivers.

Note that many high-performance digital radios use dual-point modulation to give enhanced performance and can be quite expensive due to difficulty in setting up the tracking across their working frequencies.

7.3.3 Error Protection

Within a slot, data are protected, with the exception of the synchronizing pattern, by a CCITT 16-bit CRC word. FEC, in the form of interleaved BCH (63,51) coding, is added to allow reconstruction of corrupted bits. ARQ is implemented for retransmission of packets that cannot be corrected.

7.3.4 Addressing

Mobiles each have a unique 32-bit physical identity (PID), but they are allocated MGLs at registration. The MGL is a shortened identity shared with a group of mobiles. This identity determines which of the down slots should be monitored for incoming calls. Should a packet arrive at a base station addressed to a mobile that is registered there, the base station processor looks up the MGL of that mobile and then sends the mobile's PID, a new unique MGL, and slot allocations for the transmission of the message and the amount of data to be transferred. The mobile makes an acknowledgment and proceeds to monitor the relevant slots that may be spread over several frames. An acknowledgment is sent in the assigned up slot in each frame.

If the mobile wishes to send, it first chooses one of the quarter sub-slots and makes a random access. The mobile then sends the MGL assigned to it at registration, the mobile PID, and the size of packet to be transmitted. The base acknowledgment assigns sufficient slots for the data transfer and a new MGL for labeling the data. If any data are lost in transfer due to transmission errors, the base station is able to use the acknowledgment to request retransmission and to assign further slots for transfer. Once all data have been received at the base site, the final acknowledgment back to the mobile includes the fixed network sequence number that has been assigned to the packet for onward transmission. This can be used at the mobile MMI to inform the sender that the packet is now safe in the fixed network and has a high probability of delivery. If greater security is required in a particular application, high-level acknowledgments may be included in the protocol for end-to-end signaling.

7.3.5 Terminal Interfaces

At the mobile end there are two devices available. The Messager terminal is effectively an answer-back pager unit with a miniature QWERTY keyboard, a display, and a data interface. This unit is self-contained and battery powered. The other is a radio terminating unit (RTU), which has no keypad or display, just the data interface, which is a standard V24/28 (RS232) interface that communicates at 4.8 Kbps. The physical interface uses an unusual six-pin plug arrangement.

Access to the system at the network end may be via a message server that runs Message Manager software. The server allows access to other windows applications, such as Lotus cc:Mail or a fax. The physical connection to the Cognito network is usually via a leased line to a fixed-port controller at a switching node in the network. Other arrangements are available, as shown in Figure 7.5.

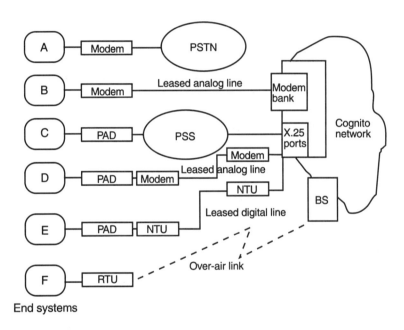

FIGURE 7.5 End system interconnection to the Cognito system.

7.3.6 System Architecture

In the U.K., the core switching network consists of eight switching sites interconnected by 64-Kbps digital lines. Each switching site has an Ethernet LAN. Intelligent switching allows rerouting between switching sites if any of the lines fail. Base stations are connected to the switching sites via landlines. Connected to the LAN at each switching site are the fixed-port controller, the directory server, the message store, the billing system, the accounting server, and the network management center.

The Cognito system has proved to be rugged; it gives good coverage both to mobiles and portables; and it is able to serve a particular segment of the market place. However, it has lacked in its ability to support, or encourage, the use of mul-

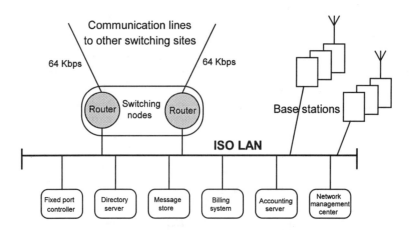

FIGURE 7.6 Cognito switching center architecture.

tiple applications due to its perceived lack of *transparency* to the data passed over it. This has been more of a marketing issue rather than one of technology.

7.4 RADIO DATA LINK ACCESS PROCEDURE

In the U.S., Motorola and IBM have been jointly running a data network primarily for IBM service personnel, with an estimated 45,000 users, called ARDIS. This network has recently been updated with higher transmission speeds and an improved over-air protocol known as radio data-link access procedure (RD-LAP). The old ARDIS network operated at a 4.8-Kbps data rate; the new one doubles this to 9.6 Kbps in a 12.5 kHz channel or 19.2 Kbps in a 25 kHz channel by means of a multilevel modulation scheme. It is claimed that the overall RF coverage has also been improved because of the addition of better coding algorithms and more efficient interleaving. The RD-LAP technology has been adopted by Deutsche Telekom Mobilfunk for their Modacom mobile data service and was to be used in the now-discontinued Hutchison Mobile Data system in the U.K.

7.4.1 Access Protocol

This system uses yet another access method called slotted digital sense multiple access (DSMA). As mentioned in the section on Paknet, this access method is one that is suitable for the transmission of multiple short random messages from a large number of subscriber units (DSMA can be regarded as a derivative of CSMA). In many respects, it is similar to the method adopted by Mobitex, except that there are no specific SILENCE or FRI telegrams to control the mobile population. The method of access is as follows:

If a mobile unit has a packet ready for transmission and the base station is transmitting a long data message, the mobile is required to wait a random time (0–50 ms) before transmission. This random time is intended to reduce the chances of a collision with a packet from another mobile that may also be ready to send since the last outbound frame synchronization sequence. If the base station is not transmitting and therefore no frame synchronization sequences are being sent, the mobile is required to wait for a period of time to seek frame synchronization before making an access attempt. The time is usually set to be slightly longer than the time of a maximum-sized outbound packet. If the mobile unit detects frame synchronization during any of the waiting times, it must wait until the end of the current outbound slot to detect the appended channel status symbol. This symbol allows the mobile to make an assessment of the likely state for the next inbound slot. If the inbound channel indicator shows IDLE, the mobile may make an immediate access attempt. If it is BUSY, the mobile must wait a random time between 0 and 700 ms before re-entering the access procedure.

A particular feature of the protocol gives preference to packet response transmissions, e.g., preference may be given to ACKs, over information packets. Figure 7.7 illustrates this.

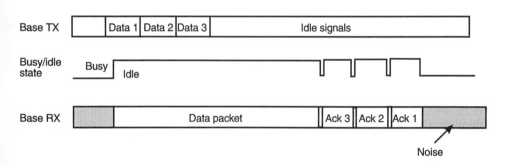

FIGURE 7.7 RD-LAP ACK stack diagram.

This specifically refers to information packets that have been network-initiated and that require acknowledgment. If a mobile receives a message and the inbound channel is known to be busy, it must wait before it makes an acknowledgment. If a second or even a third mobile receives similar packets, all active units must increment a counter to ensure that they do not respond immediately once the channel becomes free. The mobiles will thus send their acknowledgments in reverse order. Each acknowledgment slot has a duration of 45 ms. The system is programmed to a maximum mobile count, and all mobiles must be capable of incrementing to this maximum number of 10. This limits the number of confirmed service transactions emanating from a base station at any one time but allows a very ordered acknowledgment sequence.

7.4.2 Air Interface

RD-LAP uses a unique four-level FSK modulation scheme that includes Trellis coding of the symbols. The symbol rate is 4.8 kbaud, which meets the regulatory requirements for channel occupancy and adjacent channel power imposed on 12.5-kHz separated channels with a deviation of 2.2 kHz for the maximum shift symbols. The baseband data symbols are prefiltered by a square root raised cosine filter with a transition ratio of 0.2.

It is claimed that the faded C/I level, which can be used for network design purposes, is 20 dB. This makes the system marginal for a seven-cell cluster cellular design but is similar to the figures claimed for Mobitex, where successful network implementation using seven cells has been achieved. The static sensitivity of receivers for operation in the system should be at least −110 dBm for an uncorrected bit error ratio of 10^{-2}.

7.4.3 Error Protection

As with the preceding systems, the combination of CRC, block coding, interleaving, and ARQ is used with RD-LAP. In the case of RD-LAP, the header block contains 10 bytes of address and control information, to which the standard CCITT 16-bit CRC is appended. The intermediate blocks must always contain 12 bytes of user information and are protected by a four-byte CRC, which is contained in the last block. If there are insufficient data bytes to make up complete blocks then pad bytes (AAH) must be added in the last block. The number of pad bytes used is sent in the message header so that they may be easily discarded on receipt.

The last four bytes of the last block is labeled CRC2 and is a cyclic redundancy check calculated over all of the data in the intermediate blocks and the first eight bytes of the last block, including any pad bytes. It uses a generator polynomial containing 15 terms [5]. The maximum length of messages is defined as 2,048 bytes of user data for connection-oriented service and 512 bytes in the connectionless environment. However, the maximum physical length of any message is limited to 512 bytes contained in 43 data blocks, plus one address and control block, making 44 in total.

FEC is added to each 12-byte block (the header block is 10 bytes of address and control plus 2 bytes of CRC; the intermediate block contains 12 bytes of user data; and the last block contains eight bytes of data plus four bytes CRC2). All blocks are 96 bits long before coding and become 66 symbols after coding. The bits are serially grouped in threes to form 32 tri-bit symbols. A further all-zeros tri-bit symbol is appended, making 33 in all. The Trellis coder takes this 33 symbol array and transforms it into 66 four-level symbols for transmission. The algorithms [5] are too complex for discussion here but prior to transmission, the symbols are interleaved to a depth of eight. Finally, before offering the data to the modulator, each

66-symbol block is partitioned into subblocks of 22 symbols by a channel status symbol, making the total block length 69 symbols. This means that each block has a duration of $\frac{69 \text{ symbols}}{4.8 \text{ kbaud}} = 14.375$ ms.

As was done for Mobitex, the maximum effective over-air data rate may be calculated from the maximum data transfer of 512 user bytes by:

Total number of packets	=	44
Number of octets	=	512
Time taken		
(+ frame synchronization)	=	$(44 \times 14.375 \times 10^{-3}) + (14.5833 \times 10^{-3})$
Therefore, effective data rate	=	$512 \times {}^{8}\!/_{0.6470833}$
	$\cong$	6.33 Kbps

which is nearly 40% faster than Mobitex.

7.4.4 Addressing

Two bytes are reserved in the base station address field numbering plan for country codes to allow international roaming and interconnection. Appendix A [5] defines these in terms of hexadecimal numbers for most countries of the world. The logical link ID, which denotes the mobile identity on outbound messages and the address of a terminal or another mobile unit for inbound messages, is a 31-bit field. The remaining 49 bits in the header are used for control purposes.

7.4.5 Terminal Interfaces

Motorola has maintained exclusive supply of radio terminal devices to the system. Various forms of mobile data terminal (MDT) have been available for connection to standard radio products, which have a direct modulation capability. However, recently, a new product known as the Infotac has appeared on the market. It is of similar size to the Cognito Messager product but does not have a full-function keyboard. Without the addition of a terminal device, it may be regarded as a two-way pager with the ability to transmit back to the network menu-selectable preprogrammed status messages. It has sufficient memory to make it capable of storing up to about 100 such messages.

A unique feature of this product is that it uses a digital signal processor (DSP) to generate the coded modulation and can thus be reprogrammed for use on other data networks. In fact, there is a version available to operate on Mobitex networks. Like the Messager, the Infotac has a standard data interface to which terminal devices such as a laptop computer may be attached.

At the fixed end of the system, the usual array of line-connected terminals can be accommodated. However, the system architecture is such that communication between network switches is conducted via an X.25 network.

7.4.6 System Architecture

Each base station site is connected via landlines to an area communications control-ler (ACC), to which local wireline users may be connected. Other ACCs are connected via the public packet data network (PPDN) at X.25 level. Most fixed-ap-plication hosts are connected via this network.

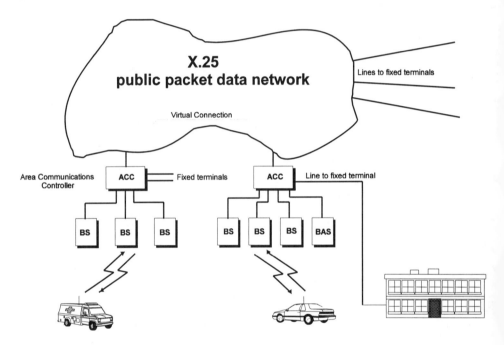

FIGURE 7.8 RD-LAP system architecture.

Initially the ACCs were proprietary switches but Sun workstations running specially developed software have proved to be both more reliable and cheaper to operate. Several of the current users have migrated to them and have found signifi-cant improvement in their systems.

Unlike Mobitex, each ACC is required to keep an account of the traffic statis-tics, the billing, and its local-area management. All roaming information must be transported through the X.25 domain for updating of databases. This increases the overhead in this area.

7.5 CONCLUSIONS

All four of the mobile data networks discussed are in current use for public access and are providing a valuable service. In terms of international acceptance, the Mobitex system is far ahead of its rivals. It does have the advantage of being one of the first, as it evolved from an indirectly modulated system at 1,200 bps in the early 1980s and was adopted by Swedish Telecom. Mobitex networks are operating in more than 20 countries and several more are planned.

Paknet and Cognito have found their niche markets in the U.K. but have failed to spread further, although various approaches have been made in the past. RD-LAP has the largest number of users on any one system in the U.S. but, with the exception of Germany, it has not made the expected impact elsewhere in the public network domain.

The net over-air data rate is highest in the case of RD-LAP, but this alone has not guaranteed success in the market place. The success of Mobitex must be viewed from the overall performance of the network, which includes all the services and facilities as well as a high level of transparency, which allows the use of custom applications. The removal of any intellectual property right (IPR) claims and the placing of the protocol in the public domain significantly helped in the early acceptance of the system. Coupled with this, the offers of assistance to would-be system integrators to produce applications suitable for the mobile scenario has contributed to its acceptance. One of its most important features is the reliability offered by the network through its redundant architecture design and its rugged modulation scheme. Speed is not everything, particularly in packet data networks.

The next public standard about to emerge into the market is TETRA, outlined in the previous chapter. Here, the effective net data rate/Hz will more than double by the use of more advanced modulation methods. However, the networks will still require particular attention for the fixed infrastructure to ensure best performance. The air interface is only one link in the chain.

With the advent of other means of data transfer, such as over GSM, PCS, and ultimately UMTS, the future of data-only systems could be looking somewhat limited, except that all of these systems should carry a cost penalty on complexity. If the true costs are passed on to the end customer, they should be higher than the dedicated data networks because the specifications currently require at least the first nodal connection to be circuit switched. This air time could be more profitably employed, carrying real-time voice information. Even when true packet data emerges on the cellular telephone networks, there will still be a customer base that does not want speech and prefers to stay with the dedicated data network as long as the cost of ownership remains competitive. It is essential that the customer base is expanded rapidly, before the other offerings are widely available. After this, it becomes more of a marketing issue than a technical one.

References

[1]   Davie, M.C., and J.B. Smith, "A Cellular Packet Radio Data Network," *Electronics & Communications Engineering Journal*, June 1991, pp.137–143.

[2]   Schoute, P.C., "Control of Aloha Signalling in a Mobile Radio Trunking System," *Proc. IEE Conference on Radio Spectrum Conservation Techniques,* London, July 1980.

[3]   The Cognito Group, "The Cognito Network Reference Guide," Newbury, England, July 1991.

[4]   ETSI, "European Radio Message System (ERMES)," ETS 300 133-1 to 133-7, 1992, Valbonne, France.

[5]   "Radio Data Link Access Procedure (RD-LAP)," Motorola Data Systems, Schaumburg, IL, March 1991.

CHAPTER 8
▼▼▼

DATA OVER CORDLESS NETWORKS

In the previous chapters we looked at data transmission over land mobile radio networks, cellular systems, and mobile data-only networks. However, there is yet another wireless system whereby data services can be deployed—cordless networks. Originally developed for the residential market for cordless phones, where the coverage area is limited to the local area, this technology has advanced through second- and third-generation systems supporting digital transmission technology with enhanced handover, roaming capabilities, etc. The core differences between cordless and cellular systems are in their coverage areas and mobility. The coverage of cordless systems is generally limited to the local area, such as within a building or a piazza. Cellular systems, as previously described, provide a much larger coverage area, which includes urban, suburban, and rural areas—these systems are usually countrywide. With regard to mobility, cordless systems tend to support only walking-speed terminals due to their limited coverage areas. With cellular systems, mobile terminals are capable of speeds up to 250 km/hr when used onboard high-speed trains.

8.1 BACKGROUND ON CORDLESS TELEPHONES

When the first cordless telephones emerged, many different systems were adopted, most of them incompatible with one another. However, most of them used analog technology with frequency modulation and frequency-division multiplex access (FDMA) channel access. These were mainly used domestically. Recently, the Conference on European Posts and Telecommunications (CEPT) has standardized what is now known as CT1+. CT1+ is an analog FDMA system accessing 80 channels in the 885–887-MHz band. It is basically the same as the former CT1 standard, except that the channels are now trunked into a common pool of channels. This standard has been accepted by most European countries but not in the U.K., due to congestion in the frequency spectrum [1].

The growing market of cordless telephones, together with the maturing of digital technology, has spawned the next generation of cordless telephones. Known as the CT2, the system was originally developed in the U.K. as the MPT 1375 standard [2] and later adopted as a pan-European standard for second-generation digital cordless telephones [3]. Using digital transmission, channel access is gained by means of FDMA and duplexing is achieved by time-division duplex (TDD). That is, uplink and downlink channels are time-divided to achieve full duplex over a single channel. There are 40 channels available in the 864–868-MHz band and the transmit power is 10 mW. The data rate achievable is 72 Kbps modulated, providing 32-Kbps duplex channels. With digital technology, it possesses features such as higher speech quality, security, and data transmission without a separate modem.

Following the introduction of CT2, CT3 or DCT 900 (DCT is an acronym for digital cordless telephones) was developed by Ericsson as a future to cordless communications. Based on a TDMA/TDD structure, it boasted *seamless* handover (achieved by maintaining the old link while setting up a new one and seamlessly handing over the connection once the new link is established) capabilities. With the incorporation of dynamic channel allocation (DCA) techniques, it supported a much higher capacity than second-generation FDMA systems. Although technically attractive, it was not adopted as a European standard. Alongside DCT 900, in 1988 the European Telecommunications Standard Institute (ETSI) started work on a European digital cordless standard, known as the Digital European Cordless Telecommunications (DECT) system. The DECT system is very similar to the DCT 900 in principle and offers a wealth of services, which will be described in the following sections.

Apart from European developments, Japan's Research and Development Center for Radio Systems (RCR) [4] initiated the personal handy phone (PHP). The Japanese PHP is very similar to DECT, taking on the TDMA/TDD transmission format. The difference between the two is the modulation technique; the former adopted the $\pi/4$-QPSK, similar to the Japanese and American digital cellular systems, and the latter adopted the GMSK technique. Table 8.1 summarizes the different cordless technologies to date.

TABLE 8.1

Summary of Cordless Technologies

System	CT2	CT3	DECT	PHP
Frequency band	864.1–868.1 MHz (Europe & Asia)	862–866 MHz (Sweden)	1.88–1.9 GHz (Europe)	1895–1907 MHz (Japan)
Multiple access	FDMA	TDMA	TDMA	TDMA
Duplexing	TDD	TDD	TDD	TDD
Modulation	GFSK	GMSK	GMSK	π/4 QPSK
Transmitted data rate	72 Kbps	640 Kbps	1152 Kbps	384 Kbps
Speech rate	32 Kbps	32 Kbps	32 Kbps	32 Kbps
Speech coding	ADPCM	ADPCM	ADPCM	ADPCM
Number of duplex slots/carrier	1	8	12	4
Channel bandwidth	100 kHz	1 MHz	1.728 MHz	300 kHz
Channel coding	No	CRC	CRC	CRC
Channel assignment	DCA	DCA	DCA	DCA

8.2 NETWORK ARCHITECTURE AND MOBILITY

Cordless systems possess very similar network architectures. To illustrate this, we will consider the DECT network infrastructure. The entities of base stations are known as radio fixed parts (RFP), and they serve a community of portable terminals known as cordless portable parts (CPP), which can be voice or data terminals. Voice connections have the link directed to the common control fixed part (CCFP), whereas the data connections are either relayed to the LAN or to the PBX, depending on the type of application. RFPs are connected via the fixed network to the CCFP, which performs the switching functions such as call routing. Attached to the CCFP are the databases, the home database (HDB) and the visitor database (VDB), which constantly monitor and update the mobility of portable terminals. Figure 8.1 illustrates.

Access to the public or private network can be gained via the PBX, which is connected to the CCFP and acts as a gateway to the global network.

One of the key issues in the design of a wireless system is the construction of a robust network infrastructure to support mobility, roaming, and security. Hierarchi-

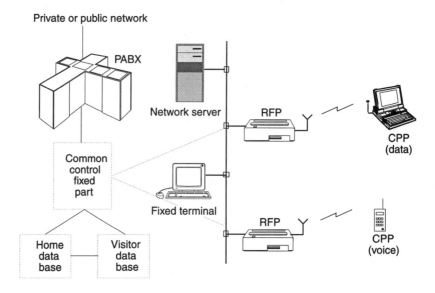

FIGURE 8.1   DECT network architecture.

cal dimensioning of a network into more manageable entities allows simpler tracking of mobile terminals. In a wireless network supporting mobility, it is essential that the location of mobile terminals be monitored for incoming calls to be routed appropriately. This requires frequent updating of terminal locations and registration into the appropriate databases. In the hierarchical dimensioning of large networks, such as a corporate or private network, smaller local networks and subnetworks can be defined. Roaming of such terminals will therefore require frequent authentication and registration, for security purposes as well as location updating. The authentication procedure generally challenges a foreign terminal with a random number generated by the network via the interrogating base station and the air interface. The terminal is then required to calculate a response based on its own identity and a *key* known to the network operator. The response generated by the terminal is then compared to that generated locally by the BS. It is valid when both are identical. The authentication procedure can also be used to check for the user's access rights to services and network facilities [5].

The design of a network is therefore crucial to the handling of security access and mobility management. The following paragraphs describe the simple design of a network and highlight some of the key issues in wireless network architectures.

The construction of a robust network architecture is achieved through the hierarchical dimensioning of the network into unique location areas and domains in the context of the network infrastructure. Location areas can be defined as the area governed by a cluster of base stations, which can be a building or a department, such as that shown in Figure 8.2. This is similar to dimensioning a network into several subnetworks. When a portable terminal enters a new location area (for example, when a terminal moves from department X to Y), it will be required to update its location. All base stations within a location area will broadcast the same identity periodically to inform portables of the domain they are entering, and the base stations may request the portable terminals to update their locations. To enable the network to track a portable's current location accurately, the procedure of location updating is required. This is necessary when a different domain is entered. Location updating information is usually stored in the HDB or VDB. When a call arrives for the portable terminal, the databases are interrogated for the exact location of the terminals before routing the call to the appropriate subnetwork. This procedure reduces the network loading from broadcast paging traffic, which would flood the network if the exact terminal location was not known. Several location areas make up a local network site, which is controlled by a common control fixed part (CCFP) with its own HDB and VDB. Private networks can further be constructed with a group of local networks, each with unique location areas. Through such a hierarchical architecture, large private networks can be created and the mobility of terminals can be managed in a controlled manner.

The management of mobility information is also an important issue, as user information, authentication procedures, and mobility management information must be exchanged over the fixed network. This covers public or private network

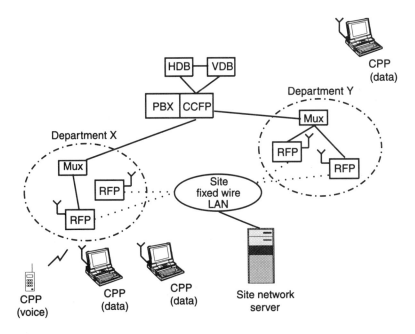

FIGURE 8.2 Hierarchical cordless network architecture.

interconnections and protocols, such as signaling system number 7 (SS7); however, we will only consider the network interconnections.

In a cordless network, interconnections between different network sites may be made via the private network or leased lines. When a portable terminal roams within its local site, it needs to update its location information with the HDB at the local network. This is mobility within the local site. When a portable terminal x belonging to site A roams to a different network site B (but still within the private network), it is required to update its location with the VDB of site B as well as its HDB back at its home at site A. This is known as intersite mobility within the private network. The procedure is required so that an incoming call for terminal x can reach terminal x while it is in site B because its precise location is stored in the HDB at its home site and the VDB at the visited site. The HDB at the visited site contains the information regarding the terminal at the visited site, while the VDB possesses the precise location of the portable terminal at the visited site.

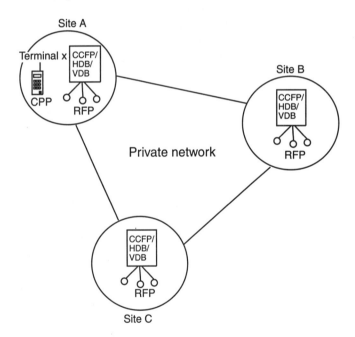

FIGURE 8.3 Interconnection of wireless network sites within a private network.

Yet another form of mobility is internetwork roaming, which introduces such issues as network security. When users of a particular private network visit a foreign network, they may find that the access rights given to them may be limited in an effort to control security. This is, of course, up to the network management, but internet access should be made available for visitors to access or retrieve information back at their corporate network. The location-updating procedures and management of information is the same as described above—the HDB at the home site keeps a record of the address of the visited site, while the VDB at the visited site keeps track of the portable location at the foreign site.

Mobility management is a complex issue altogether. In planning a high-density wireless network, the design of the fixed network is vital to the success of the network. Issues such as user traffic patterns, frequency of handovers, teletraffic, and network congestion must be considered. Further insight into this subject is provided in [6–8].

8.3 DATA SERVICES

Cordless systems such as CT2 and DECT have been developed with voice as the primary application. However, as the technology matures, interest is growing in mobile data applications such as wireless faxing, data terminal emulation, video, and cordless interconnection to the ISDN and LANs. The business environment is a target for cordless systems because of the high mobility of users. Hence, most of the services are aimed at the office environment. We have heard of the concept of the paperless office through advancement in computer communications, electronic mail, and electronic document formats such as electronic data interchange (EDI). With cordless systems in place in the office environment, voice and data terminals are no longer bound to wires and cables, introducing the new concept of the cordless office.

8.4 CT2

The FDMA-structured CT2 system supports asynchronous and synchronous data services on the 32-Kbps duplex channels, in addition to adaptive differential pulse code modulation (ADPCM) coded voice. The bandwidth available provides circuit mode (connection-oriented) data bearer services at data rates of 300; 1,200; 2,400; 4,800; 9,800; 14,400; 19,200; and 32,000 (synchronous mode only with no error protection) bps.

One may argue that 32 Kbps is inadequate for the provision of data services. Studies and simulations have shown that even on a 32-Kbps radio channel access into an Ethernet LAN (based on the DECT system), low-bit-rate data applications for portable data terminals, such as e-mail and remote terminal login, can be supported quite comfortably [9]. Typical applications expected for CT2 include wireless data terminals, fax, and, in the future, low-bit-rate video telephony. As previously described in Chapters 3 and 4, the indoor radio channel is quasistatic in nature, with long average duration of fades. This effectively causes large error bursts to the data stream. Hence, sufficient error control must be built into the application. Depending on the type of service, poor error rates may be tolerable because the information may still be intelligible.

Service types can be categorized into synchronous and asynchronous. In general, synchronous-type applications are those that are time-critical. Such services need to satisfy the timing requirements of the fixed network. An example is the interworking with the public switched telephone network (PSTN) and the integrated services digital network (ISDN). Propagation and protocol delays must therefore be minimized. On the other hand, asynchronous-type applications do not have timing restrictions, so they are not too sensitive to delays. Typical asynchronous-type services include packet-mode applications, such as LANs.

The CT2 standard in Europe has been proposed to support data services using Reed Solomon (RS) forward error correction (FEC) and ARQ for asynchronous services to ensure data integrity [3]. The asynchronous data service components are shown in Figure 8.4.

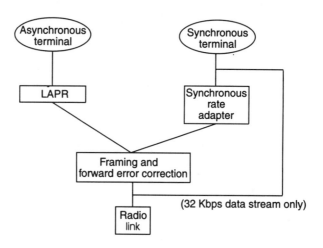

FIGURE 8.4 Data service components in CT2.

Asynchronous data has additional error control in the form of ARQ to ensure data integrity. This is the link access protocol for radio (LAPR). The LAPR is based on the high-level data link control (HDLC) frame format and the frames are protected with FEC prior to transmission. For synchronous applications, the data streams are synchronously rate-adapted to one of the standard rates mentioned earlier (except for the 32-Kbps transparent data service). These formatted frames are then reformatted and coded with RS FEC codewords, as with asynchronous data services. The RS code specified in the CT2 standard is represented by the notation (n,k;d) where n is the block length, k is the number of information symbols, and d is the number of symbols reserved for error detection. The code for CT2 takes on the general form of (63,k;3) with eight-bit symbols. The factor k can be 2, 4, 6, 11, 21, 30, or 40, which represents user bit rates of 300; 1,200; 2,400; 4,800; 9,600; 14,400; and 19,200. The formatted FEC frames are transmitted synchronously in eight 1-msec bursts, spanning a period of 16 ms. The FEC frame consists of an eight-bit synchronization word followed by a 504-bit RS codeword. The RS FEC uses eight-bit symbols; hence, the RS codeword is made up of 63 eight-bit symbols, k of which carries user data and 63-k of which are made up of parity symbols. The FEC frame structure is shown in Figure 8.5.

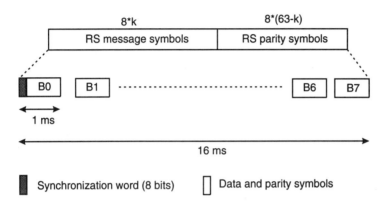

FIGURE 8.5 CT2 FEC frame structure.

In a similar system in Canada, known as the CT2Plus, RS codes have also been specified [10] for error-correction coding with data transmission. The main difference between the two systems is the number of bits per symbol used. In the CT2Plus system, six-bit symbols are used, while the European CT2 uses eight-bit symbols. Consequently, the FEC frames are transmitted in six 1-msec bursts over a 12-ms frame period. The FEC codeword in the CT2 Plus system is therefore 384 bits in total, with the first six bits of the 12-ms frame reserved for synchronization and the remaining 378 bits reserved for the 63 six-bit RS symbols.

8.5 THE CT2 INDOOR RADIO PROPAGATION CHANNEL

To study the performance of data transmission over the CT2 system, indoor radio propagation measurements were conducted at various indoor environments, with mobile and static terminals, at furnished and unfurnished locations [11].

Bit-error vector measurements—bit-by-bit error vectors recorded for a pseudo random binary sequence (PRBS) data stream—were performed with an HP 3780 data generator/error detector, a commercially available CT2 handset and base station (modified to transmit data transparently into the burst mode controller of the handset for transmission), and a data logger. The average BERs in some of the measurement runs varied between 1×10^{-5} to 4×10^{-2}, depending on the environment and movement of the terminal (whether it is static or mobile).

8.6 PERFORMANCE OF RS CODES ON THE CT2 SYSTEM

Based on the bit-error vectors collected from the radio channel measurements indoors, the performance of RS codes were simulated and studied. The simulation model adopted is shown in Figure 8.6. A PRBS data generator feeds pseudo random sequences into the RS encoder, which performs the coding at the rates specified in the standard. The codewords generated are then *corrupted* by the radio channel that is represented by the bit-error vectors recorded in the indoor radio channel. At the receiver, the codewords are then decoded appropriately and compared with the original PRBS sequence transmitted for uncorrected or residual errors.

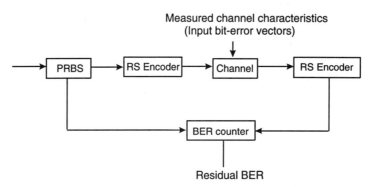

FIGURE 8.6 Simulation model to study the performance of RS codes.

The performance of the RS codes in the radio channel are plotted in Figure 8.7 with the residual BER (after error correction) against the measured channel characteristics (before error correction). For channel BERs of less than 1.5×10^{-5}, no residual errors were present. For measurement runs selected in this study (with an average BER of 7×10^{-3}), in most instances residual errors were found to be present, even with FEC.

The error characteristics used in the study may not be typical; however, they may be encountered. The error characteristics are highly dependent on the environment, the building structure (the measurement experiments mentioned here were carried out in a predominantly steel building, which is not the best environment for radio signal propagation!), the equipment used (implementation), etc. From the measurements and simulations, it can be concluded that for the provision of synchronous services in the CT2 system, the residual error rates present will require that applications must tolerate errors in most instances. In *image*-type applications, such as fax or video, low residual errors present may not corrupt the intelligibility of the image and hence may be able to survive the transmission. For data transfer applications, such as wireless data terminals, hybrid ARQ with LAPR and FEC will be required to guarantee data integrity, but will limit the service to an asynchronous one. This does not really affect applications such as e-mail or remote login, where the nature of data transfer is asynchronous. Asynchronous facsimile standards are already emerging in the U.S. [12] to enable the direct connection of new fax machines with digital output to mobile terminals. In addition, fax packet assembler/disassemblers (PAD) are being developed to enable fax transmission through packet networks.

8.7 DECT

The DECT system was developed as a single enhanced cordless system for Europe. It possesses advanced technical features that support a wealth of services [13]. Its technical features include dynamic channel allocation (DCA), which supports high capacity and eliminates the need for frequency planning. DCA, a technique of assigning channels dynamically based on a set of criteria such as the level of interference and received signal strength, supports portable-controlled seamless handover, as well as inter- and intracell handovers (handovers performed within a cell to a better quality channel) [14,15]. DCA is adaptive to traffic and eliminates the need for frequency planning.

In addition to these advanced technical capabilities, DECT provides an environment that supports integrated services such as voice, data, ISDN fax, video, and wireless LANs.

8.8 FLEXIBLE FRAME STRUCTURE

The TDMA/TDD frame structure used in DECT supports a total of 24 slots, the first 12 of which are allocated to downlink and the remainder to uplink. In addition, half slots and double slots are also defined. All of the different slot types contain a fixed-length field for control and signaling and a variable data field. The double slot supports the highest data rate, while the half slot supports the lowest. Each slot exists in protected and unprotected formats; the former incorporates additional error protection for error-sensitive services such as data [16]. The general DECT slot and frame structure is shown in Figure 8.7.

In the protected slots, the B field is further divided into B_n subfields of 80 bits, where 64 bits are allocated to user information and 16 bits are allocated to the cyclic redundancy check (CRC). The number of subfields for the half, full, and double slots are 1, 4, and 10, respectively, providing a total data rate of 80, 320, and 800 bits in the user data or B-field.

8.9 CONNECTION TYPES

To allow for an integrated-services environment supporting applications at various data rates, DECT provides the ability to combine the bandwidth of several time

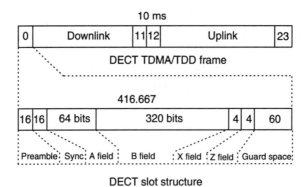

DECT slot structure

FIGURE 8.7 DECT slot and frame structures.

slots to achieve a high bit-rate connection. The combination of multiple time slots is also known as *multibearer connections*. To enable multibearer connections to use the available bandwidth more efficiently, symmetric and asymmetric connections are available. In applications where data traveling in one direction is higher than the other—such as fax—using a duplex connection will be inefficient in its usage of bandwidth. Multibearer symmetric and asymmetric connections can be set up through multiple-simplex or duplex bearers, the connection type depending on the requirements of the applications. For definition, a double-simplex bearer is created when both time slots of a pair are used for transmission in one direction, while in a conventional duplex bearer, the paired slots are operated in opposite directions. Figure 8.8 illustrates the different bearer types.

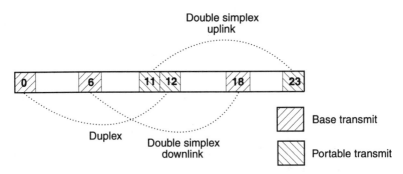

FIGURE 8.8 The various bearer connection types in DECT.

Symmetric connections will therefore always have identical traffic bearers in both uplink and downlink directions, whereas in asymmetric connections, the traffic will be higher in one direction than it will be in the other. Asymmetric connections will compose of both duplex and double-simplex bearers (in a connection, at least one duplex bearer must be assigned for control information or acknowledgments to be relayed back to the originator).

8.10 SERVICES

DECT allows the combination of simplex and duplex bearers to form multibearers of higher bandwidth for the provision of higher bit-rate services. The services defined in the standard include support for the PSTN, ISDN interconnection, fax, video, X.25, LAN, and interworking with GSM [17,18].

The support of these services is possible through the combination of slot types (full, half, or double), the number of slots, and the slot formats (protected or unprotected). The environment for the creation of services is therefore very much a pick 'n' mix one, whereby services and applications can be implemented through combining different slot types and formats.

A typical set of voice and data services and their requirements, slot types, connections, and formats are shown in Table 8.2. The table is based on full slots, protected formats (for data), and unprotected (for voice), at 25.6 Kbps and 32 Kbps per slot, respectively.

TABLE 8.2

Mapping Services to Slots

Service	Connection Type	Slot Format	Slot Type	Uplink/ Downlink Slot Ratio	Total Number of Slots	Allocated User Bit Rate
32-Kbps voice	S	U	1 full-slot duplex	1/1	2	32 Kbps
9.6-Kbps fax	S	P	1 full-slot duplex	1/1	2	25.6 Kbps
64-Kbps fax	A	P	1 full-slot duplex + 1 full-slot double simplex	3/1	4	76.8 Kbps
64-Kbps video	S	P	3 full-slot duplex	3/3	6	76.8 Kbps
256-Kbps LAN	A	P	1 full-slot duplex + 5 full-slot double simplex	11/1	12	281.6 Kbps

TABLE 8.2 (continued)

Service	Connection Type	Slot Format	Slot Type	Uplink/ Downlink Slot Ratio	Total Number of Slots	Allocated User Bit Rate
2B + D ISDN at 144 Kbps	S	P	6 full-slot duplex	6/6	12	153.6 Kbps
1 B + D ISDN at 80 Kbps	S	P	4 full-slots duplex	4/4	8	102.4 Kbps

8.11 CHANNEL CONDITIONS

The channel characteristics of DECT are no different than those of CT2. The DECT environment suffers from large signal variations due to multipath causing error bursts, such as the one shown in Figure 3.6, which reveals the quality of a typical DECT radio channel and signal fluctuations encountered. The error characteristics, detailed in the early chapters of this book, are of particular importance in the design of error-control techniques for data transmission.

Because DECT is a wideband system, delay spread is a major concern to the channel quality due to time-dispersion effects. Studies on the DECT radio channel were conducted on the U.K. DECT test bed for the effect of delay spreads on the channel quality.

With the criterion of the maximum acceptable BER as 10^{-3}, simulations were carried out to determine the maximum tolerable delay spread. Without diversity, the critical BER was exceeded when the delay spread was greater than 91 ns, which is limited in some DECT-targeted application environments. [19,20]. However, with diversity implementation, this can be extended to 178 ns and 260 ns (for 20 and 60 dB, respectively). On another DECT test bed [21–23] set up to investigate the effects of time dispersion, it was also observed that delay spread is a limiting factor on the channel quality and that antenna diversity in receivers would be required. Data from this latter test bed have been used in most of the simulations carried out in the study of the performance of DECT services, and will be described in the following sections. The test bed consists of a transmitter and receiver with a direct conversion structure [24,25], an error-measurement unit, and a PC to perform the control of measurements. The transmitter and receiver were linked by a natural radio channel of defined delay spread, with no line of sight between the transmitter and receiver. Figure 8.9 illustrates the measurement setup.

The error-measurement unit checks for synchronization and bit errors. Synchronization errors are recorded as either pass or fail (0 or 1), and bit errors are logged as the total number of errors in the B field. They are then combined as the

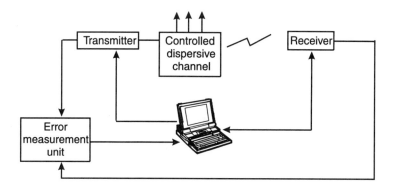

FIGURE 8.9 The measurement setup.

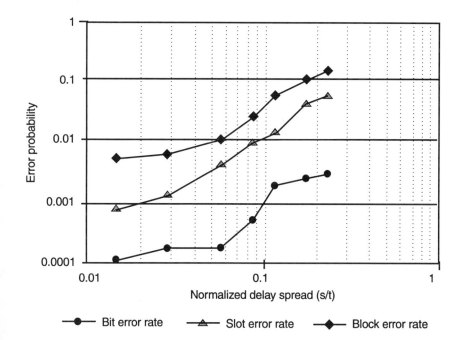

FIGURE 8.10 Typical measured indoor radio channel characteristics.

overall block-error rate. An example of a bit, slot, and overall block-error rate measured in a radio channel is shown in Figure 8.10.

It can be observed that the channel BERs are high, often corrupting half of the packet. Hence, FEC techniques operating in such environments will not be efficient. ARQ is the better choice to ensure data integrity. ARQ techniques guarantee data integrity; however, they suffer from protocol delays, which increase relative to the channel-error rate. This effectively limits the provision of services to asynchronous-type services. In DECT, however, the use of fixed and variable throughput services [26] enables the provision of synchronous- and asynchronous-type services.

8.12   SERVICES ON DECT

Fixed-throughput services ensure that the end-to-end delivery of frames is maintained at all times. This is accomplished through the introduction of a lifetime on the packets, which ensures that after a certain time period, frames that are still in error will be delivered to the higher layers, regardless of the status of the packet. Although this ensures a constant throughput (hence supporting synchronous-type applications), data integrity is not guaranteed. Variable-throughput services, on the other hand, guarantee data integrity by retransmitting frames until they are received correctly. However, they are limited to the provision of nontime-critical or asynchronous services.

8.13   STUDY OF THE PERFORMANCE OF SERVICES OVER DECT

Since the development of the DECT standard, there has been considerable interest in the ability of DECT to support an integrated-services environment. One of the earlier studies involved the performance of typical portable applications for wireless LANs, such as e-mail, telnet (remote terminal login), and file transfer protocol (FTP), a protocol commonly used for transferring and receiving files. Using a single 32-Kbps duplex DECT time slot, the different applications were simulated over a typical radio link [9]. The simulation involved a portable terminal gaining access to a LAN via a DECT radio link, through a base station attached to a LAN. In this scenario, the portable terminal behaves as if it was a terminal attached to the LAN. ARQ error control was used to ensure that data integrity was achieved on the radio link, and the objective of the simulations was to study the ARQ error control and the additional time delays introduced on the application by it and the 32-Kbps link.

The results indicated that for interactive terminal applications such as telnet and e-mail, a single 32-Kbps link could comfortably support such applications. However, for FTP, the delays encountered through the limited bandwidth of the connection increase considerably with the file size.

The relative performance of higher bit-rate applications, such as fax, video, and LAN (fixed terminals), with multibearers were studied for the number of slots or bandwidth required. A multibearer simulator performed end-to-end error control with selective repeat (SR) and go back N (GBN) ARQ [27,28]. Full slots were used throughout the simulations. The packet structure used is shown in Figure 8.11.

Out of the 320 bits in the B field, one bit is used for acknowledgment information (in the figure, A is used for positive acknowledgments, N is used for negative

64 bits	8	1	8	9	1	277	16
A Field	N(s)	A/N	N(r)	Len	M	User Data	CRC

FIGURE 8.11 A packet structure for use in multibearers.

acknowledgments); eight bits each are used for the send and receive sequence numbers, N(s) and N(r) respectively; nine bits are used for the length field, Len; one bit is used for fragmentation (M, for More); and 16 bits are used for the CRC. A total of 43 bits are overhead, leaving 277 bits per slot for user information. This effectively allows a single full slot a throughput of 27.7 Kbps.

Services such as the 9.6-Kbps and 64-Kbps fax, video at 64 Kbps, and a 256-Kbps LAN service were among the applications considered in the multibearer simulations. Table 8.3 summarizes the service characteristics and slot requirements.

TABLE 8.3
Multibearer Services and Their Requirements

Service Type	Connection Type	Multibearer Type	Number of Slots	Data Rates Achievable
9.6-Kbps fax	Asymmetric	1/1	2	~ 28 Kb
64-Kbps fax	Asymmetric	3/1, 5/1	4, 6	~ 84,140 Kb
64-Kbps video	Symmetric	3/3, 4/4	6, 8	~ 84,112 Kb
256-Kbps LAN	Asymmetric	9/1, 11/1	10, 12	~ 252,308 Kb

8.14 FAX

Currently, most fax terminals use the Group 3 (G3) fax transmission algorithm at 9.6 Kbps. In addition, there are Group 4 (G4) faxes at 64 Kbps [29] and the proposed G3 fax at 64 Kbps [30]. Transmitted fax pages are typically around 128 Kb in size and take approximately 30 seconds with G3 transmission over the wired medium. However, due to the characteristics of the radio medium, the transmission time will be longer. The G3 fax algorithm uses Modified Huffman encoding, which statistically encodes lines depending on the run-lengths of the pixels. Each line is encoded independently, unlike G4 fax, which uses Modified Read encoding. Modified Read encoding codes lines based on the difference between the current and the previous line. Although G4 fax is more efficient, errors propagate through the page due to the nature of the coding algorithm. Fax services typically have unidirectional data transfer characteristics and hence will be more spectrally efficient with asymmetric channels.

G3 fax and G4 fax (and possibly high-speed G3 fax at 64 Kbps) were simulated, and the results obtained are shown in Figure 8.12. A 1-1 symmetric connection would be sufficient for the modest 9.6-Kbps fax service. Because fax-traffic characteristics are predominantly unidirectional, for the 64-Kbps fax service, a 3-1 (three uplink-one downlink connection type, made up of one duplex and one double-simplex bearers) asymmetric connection would provide for the service, as long as the delay spread of the channel does not exceed 200 ns. However, a 5-1 (made up of one duplex and two double-simplex bearers) connection would comfortably cater for this service.

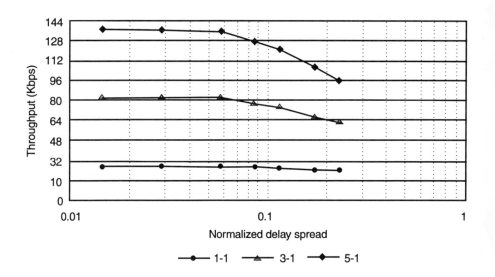

FIGURE 8.12 Fax service over DECT multibearers.

8.15 VIDEO

With the advancing developments of image-compression algorithms, there has been a growing interest in mobile video telephony applications. We chose 64 Kbps as the $n \times$ 64-Kbps H.261 standard for video telephony and a codec under study for mobile video transmission. The codec chosen for the simulations is found in [31]. A reasonable mobile videophone service can be achieved with eight bits/pixel grayscale images coded in a monochrome format of 176×144 pixels at a frame refresh rate of five frames per second (the first frame is coded using intraframe coding and the subsequent frame with interframe coding; information from previous frames are used to reduce the coding rate). Two types of image sequences are used, one has action and the other, mainly static. These sequences (of five frames each) are 54 Kb and 21 Kb in size, respectively. This essentially requires three to four duplex symmetric connections. Figure 8.13 illustrates the performance of a 64-Kbps monochrome video service using three and for symmetric multibearers. As observed with fax, the throughput starts to degrade at 50 ns. For a 3-3 duplex connection, and at large delay spread of 200 ns, the throughput falls below that required. Therefore, a 4-4 duplex connection may be more appropriate. In addition, when the channel quality degrades, the number of frame refreshes may decrease, producing a more jerky image (in action sequences). This is to cope and compensate for the decrease in throughput if no additional slots are available.

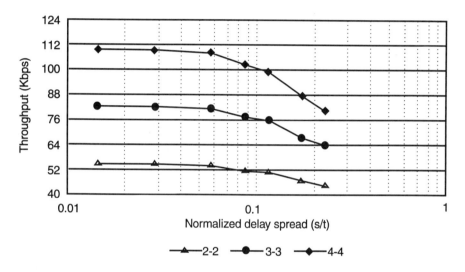

FIGURE 8.13 Portable video service over multibearers.

In a wireless video conference demonstration put on by British Telecom Laboratories in the U.K., full-motion color video transmission using the H.261 image-compression standard was successfully transmitted over the DECT radio link [32,33]. The experiments confirmed that error correction was most effective with ARQ in the DECT channel. Also, interleaving techniques were not seen as a good solution to error bursts, as interleaving spreads errors over more blocks, which resulted in more blocks being transmitted in addition to interleaving delays.

8.16 LAN SERVICE

For higher bit-rate LAN applications, the use of multibearer connections in the DECT system has been simulated to support a higher bit-rate LAN service. Taking 256 Kbps as the minimum bit rate supported by a wireless LAN service (this is tabulated as Category 1 of the ETSI Radio LAN Standardization Program, detailed in

Chapter 9), we consider the asymmetric multibearer connection, where 11 uplink slots and one downlink slot (or 11-1) are used because data are often transferred asymmetrically in a LAN. Simulations were carried out for the asymmetric connections and the results are shown in Figure 8.14.

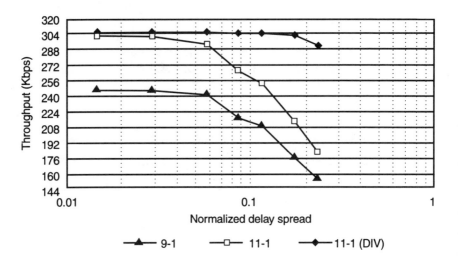

FIGURE 8.14   Multibearer 256-Kbps LAN service.

To achieve 256 Kbps, when the 11-1 connection is used, the throughput starts to degrade at a delay spread of 50 ns, falling below the minimum of 256 Kbps at around 100 ns. Without any implementation of diversity, this is clearly insufficient for the provision of a wireless LAN service. With diversity, the throughput increases considerably and remains stable close to the maximum throughput until 150 ns, when it starts to degrade. Based on this observation it is advisable for multibearer connections to implement antenna diversity to improve the throughput performance.

To investigate the performance of a LAN service further, a typical file transfer transaction was simulated. File sizes between 20 KB and 400 KB were transferred over an Ethernet using the TCP/IP based file transfer protocol (FTP). The total transaction details were captured using network monitoring software and then simulated over the DECT multibearer connections. The performance of multibearer asymmetric connections with 9-1 and 11-1 combinations were compared to that on a fixed wire Ethernet connection. The results, illustrated in Figure 8.15, show that the delay in file transfers are in the region of approximately twice the overall transaction time over the Ethernet. Of course, when considering such an application, we must bear in mind that the available bandwidth of the multibearer asymmetric connections is only a small fraction of the available bandwidth on the Ethernet.

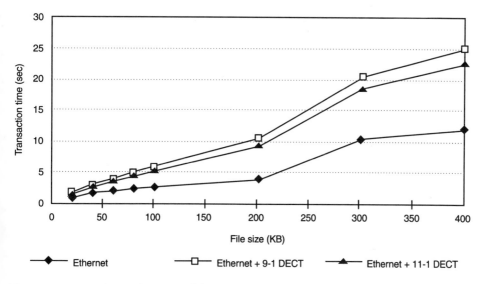

FIGURE 8.15 File transfer over multibearer connections.

8.17 CONCLUSIONS

Cordless systems have great potential to be the provider of integrated voice and data services for the wireless office environment. Various issues, such as standards, error control considerations, network architectures, and channel characteristics, related to data services over cordless systems have been addressed in this chapter.

The services described represent only a small range of the potential applications, and the full capabilities of cordless systems still remain to be exploited in the deployment of future mobile data services.

References

[1] Wong, P., "Developments of Mobile Communications Systems in Europe," *Proceedings Journal of the Institution of Engineers*, Malaysia, December 1993.

[2] U.K. Department of Trade and Industry, "Common Air Interface Specification to be Used for the Interworking between Cordless Telephone Apparatus," performance specification, MPT 1375, London, May 1989.

[3] ETSI, "Common Air Interface Specification to be Used for the Interworking Between Cordless Telephone Apparatus in the Frequency Band 864.1 to 868.1 MHz, Including Public Access Services," Draft I-ETS 300-131, Valbonne, France, 1991.

[4] Kuramoto, M., "Development of a Digital Cellular System and a Digital Cordless Telephone System in Japan," *Proc. IEEE International Conference on Wireless Communications '92*, 1992, pp. 6–9.

[5]   ETSI, *Digital European Cordless Telecommunications Common Interface Part 6: Identities and Addressing*, ETS 300 175-6, Valbonne, France, October 1992.

[6]   Jabbari, B., "Intelligent Network Concepts in Mobile Communications," *IEEE Communications Magazine*, Vol. 30, No. 2, February 1992, pp. 64–69.

[7]   Goodman, D.J., "Intelligent Mobility Management for Personal Communications", *IEE Colloquium on Mobility Management in Support of Personal Communications*, Digest 1993/151, London, June 1993, pp. 4/1–4.

[8]   Apfelbeck, J., K. Georgokitsos, and K.A. Turban, "UMTS Mobility Management," *IEE Electronic and Communications Engineering Journal*, Vol. 5, No. 3, June 93, pp. 159–164.

[9]   Wong, P., and F. Halsall, "Data Applications for DECT," *Proceedings IEEE ICC '93*, Geneva, Switzerland, May 1993, pp. 1,274–1,278.

[10] Jalali, A., G. Mony, and L. Strawczynski, "Performance of Data Protocols for In-Building Wireless System," *Proceedings IEEE International Conference on Universal Personal Communications '92*, Ottawa, Canada, 1992, pp. 407–411.

[11] Wong, P., J.R. Davis, J.F. Savage, N. Allen, and F. Halsall, "The Performance of the CT2 System for Data Services," *Proc. IEEE Vehicular Technology Conference 94*, Stockholm, Sweden, June 7–11, 1994.

[12] Weisman, D., A.H. Levesque, and R.A. Dean, "Interoperable Wireless Data," *IEEE Communications Magazine*, February 1993, pp. 69–77.

[13] van der Hoek, Hans, "The New DECT Standard for Cordless Communications," *Telecommunications*, February 1993, pp. 77–80.

[14] ETSI, "Digital European Cordless Telecommunications Reference Document," ETR 015.

[15] ETSI, "A Guide to DECT Features that Influence the Traffic Capacity and the Maintenance of High Radio Link Transmission Quality Including the Results of Simulations", ETR 042, July 1992.

[16] ETSI, "Digital European Cordless Telecommunications Common Interface Part 3: Medium Access Control Layer," ETS 300 175-3, October 1992.

[17] ETSI, "DECT System Description Document," ETSI Draft European Technical Report Version 3.4, DR/RES 3004, June 1992.

[18] ETSI, DECT Common Interface Services and Facilities Requirements Specification, Valbonne, France, March 1992.

[19] Wilkinson, T.A., "Channel Modelling and Link Simulation Studies for the DECT Test Bed Program," *Proc. 6th IEE International Conference on Mobile Radio and Personal Communications*, IEE Conference Record 351, Warwick, U.K., Dec. 1991, pp. 293–299.

[20] Wilkinson, T.A., "Link Simulation Studies for the DECT Test Bed," EC-COST 231 TD (91) 49.

[21] Schultes, G., W. Simbürger, H. Novak, and M. Happl, "Physical and Medium Access Layer DECT Test Bed", COST 231 TD (92) 28.

[22] Schultes, G., J. Fuhl, and R. Gahleitner, "Error Performance of a DECT Link with Delay-less Antenna Switching Diversity," COST 231TD(92)98.

[23] Schultes, G., A.L. Scholtz, M. Happel, and W. Simbürger, "A Testbed for DECT Physical and Medium Access Layers," *Proceedings 3rd IEEE International Symposium on PIMRC*, Boston, Oct. 19–21 1992, pp. 349–355.

[24] Schultes, G., A.L. Scholtz, E. Bonek, and P. Veith, "A New Incoherent Direct Conversion Receiver," *Proc. 40th IEEE Vehicular Technology Conference*, Orlando, FL, May 1990, pp. 668–674.

[25] Schultes, G., E. Bonek, A. Scholtz, and P. Kreuzgruber, "Low-Cost Direct Conversion Receiver Structures for TDMA Mobile Radio and Personal Communications," IEE Conf. Record 351, Warwick, U.K., Dec. 1991, pp. 143–150.

[26] ETSI, "Digital European Cordless Telecommunications Common Interface Part 4: Data Link Control Layer," ETS 300 175-4, Valbonne, France, October 1992.

[27] Wong, P., A. Lasa, F. Halsall, and G. Schultes, "Performance of Multi-bearer Connections for Varied Data Services in a TDMA System," *Proceedings of IEEE ICC 94*, New Orleans, LA, May 1–5, 1994.

[28] Lasa, A., "Data Transmission over DECT," M.Sc. Thesis, University of Swansea, U.K., 1993.

[29] McConnel, K.R., D. Bodson, and R. Schaphorst, *FAX: Digital Facsimile Technology and Applications*, Second Edition, Norwood, MA: Artech House, 1992.

[30] Costello, J., "Will Politics Rule the Fax Revolution?" *Communications International*, March 1993, pp. 41–44.

[31] Vaisey, J., E. Yuen, and J. Cavers, "Video Coding for Very High Rate Mobile Data Transmission," *Proc. IEEE VTC '92*, 1992, pp. 259–262.

[32] Heron A., and N. MacDonald, "Proceedings IEE International Conference on Image Processing and its Applications," *IEE Conference Publication 354*, April 7–9, 1992, Maastricht, The Netherlands, pp. 621–624.

[33] Fletcher, P., "DECT Standard Demo Puts Full Motion Video over Cordless Telephone Link," *Electronic Design, September 17, 1992, pp. 34*.

CHAPTER 9

▼▼▼

MOBILE DATA WITH WIRELESS LANS

The current trend in the personal computer (PC) industry points towards a steady growth in portable computers [1], and studies have shown that portable PC sales have overtaken those of conventional desktop PCs. This will create a demand for access into the fixed network for services and facilities. Currently, access is either through *docking stations*, whereby the portable PC slots either into a shell similar to a conventional desktop PC with a LAN connection or into a LAN adapter that enables communication via the parallel port or via the Personal Computer Memory Card International Association (PCMCIA) slot into the LAN, provided a node on the LAN is available. Although this provides a solution to network access, it creates the problem of requiring an available node for access into the LAN. However, with recent advances in digital radio communications, high-speed data communications is possible, enabling access into the LAN via a wireless radio link. This is the wireless LAN, whereby access to network services and applications is no longer gained by conventional wired media but instead by a wireless radio link. This revolutionizes the concept of local network computing introduced just more than a decade ago.

9.1 WHY WIRELESS LANs?

Very often, companies shuffle their personnel about [2]. This means moving telephones, computers, etc. Studies have shown that every computer or terminal in an

---

office is moved an average of 1.5 to 3 times a year. There is also a need for note-book PCs to have short-term or temporary access to the LAN for file transfers, net-work printing, or e-mail communications. Using radio avoids the inconvenience of waiting for a connection and the high cost of rewiring. Furthermore, temporary of-fice sites can be set up with ease, enabling access to all network services required.

Cable replacement or wireless access is just a small fraction of the potential of wireless LANs. The introduction of the *computer-on-a-chip* [3], has given rise to personal digital assistants (PDA) and the rapid developments of personal portable computers. These small and highly portable computers will demand access into the wireless network [4]. The ability to access the network anywhere will introduce a wide range of applications offering personal mobile computing services.

9.2 THE APPLICATIONS

Within wireless LAN systems, there are two main categories—untethered and port-able—and they have different application scenarios. In the former, the application is restricted to local on-premise networking, usually bound to the desk. The latter, however, supports portability and roaming features, as well as ubiquitous coverage.

9.2.1 Untethered Applications

Untethered or cable replacement systems are more suitable for equipment that is not portable or is usually static, such as workstations, desktop computers, and servers. However, these applications are more demanding of bandwidth. Some typical appli-cations are in the office environment, where there are an abundance of graph-ics/CAD terminals, i.e., X-windows workstations. These usually demand large bandwidths in the order of MHz. A further application is program loading/sharing, which has medium-to-large bandwidth demands, considering the size of commercial software these days. The substitution of cable also avoids the unsightly mess of "spaghetti" connections that frequently occur in offices due to connection to peripher-als such as printers and plotters and connections to LANs, WANs, and modems.

However, portability or mobility is often not required of the terminals running these applications, as they are mostly static, except for the occasional office and equipment reshuffle.

9.2.2 Portable Applications

In the area of portable applications, the following scenario is envisaged. Executives arriving at a board meeting with their notebook PCs log into the LAN at the corpo-rate network headquarters using radio for access into files and spreadsheets, which are being discussed at the meeting. Copies of reports for circulation can be printed on the network printer, enabling the executive to travel light. Documents can also be retrieved before the meeting or downloaded after the discussions, providing easier handling of data.

The retail market is also an area where portable LAN access has the potential to capture, for example, point-of-sale terminals or inventory control. [5]. In the manufacturing environment, wireless LANs can support industrial automation. Offices or service areas that are not within vicinity of the plant information system can use wireless connections to bridge the gap, enabling portable terminals to monitor and control while roaming onsite. Hence, industrial robots, automated guided vehicles (AGV), transducers, and programmable logic controllers can be operated and monitored from a different area [6]. These applications produce short transactions, typically 100 bytes.

9.3 CONCEPT OF THE WIRELESS LAN

Wireless LANs are essentially access technologies using a radio link to connect to the fixed local network. Hence, the construction of a wireless LAN will rely on the existing backbone network, such as the token ring. A typical wireless LAN configuration is shown in Figure 9.1. Portable or cordless terminals are linked to the network (in this example, an Ethernet) via the radio link. These terminals can be called the cordless portable parts (CPP), and they gain access to the fixed-wire LAN via the radio base stations or the radio fixed parts (RFP). The RFPs are fixed wireless transceivers attached to the fixed network and provide microcellular radio coverage to portable and cordless terminals. Wireless LANs can also be configured to link segments of a LAN together, functioning as a radio bridge, as shown in Figure 9.2.

In this configuration, the wireless transceivers, which normally function as a CPP, communicate and convey the traffic from various LAN segments onto the trunk via the RFP. The RFP will not only serve the LAN segment, but will provide access for other portable terminals as well.

9.4 EXPECTATIONS OF A WIRELESS LAN SYSTEM

In order for wireless LANs to gain a share of the already booming LAN market, they must satisfy most user expectations. User expectations in general are high in wireless LAN terms, such as bandwidth requirements. The radio spectrum is a scarce resource and is often difficult for a wireless service in the range of frequencies below 2 GHz to support 10-Mbps transmissions to equal that of a LAN.

Ubiquitous coverage is another factor and is sometimes difficult and costly to achieve indoors, where the transmit power is low and the radio signal has to propagate through walls. The propagation environment, as mentioned in Chapter 3, is crucial to radio coverage, especially indoors, where the density of furniture, personnel, and wall and building structure limit the coverage distance. In addition to uniform coverage, mobility is a growing demand, and users will expect seamless or

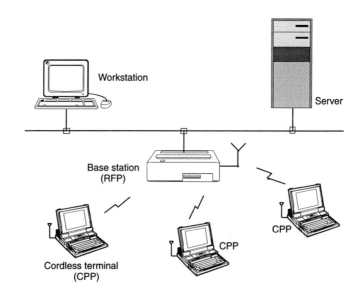

FIGURE 9.1 Typical wireless LAN configuration.

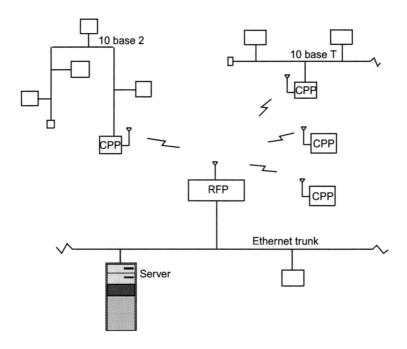

FIGURE 9.2 Wireless LAN system configured as a bridge.

transparent handover between cells and networks. Capacity is also a requirement, so that when a system is loaded the network does not experience noticeable delays.

Another criterion is network flexibility, which includes the ability of a network to adapt to reconfigurations. In addition, the ability of the network to support integrated voice, data, and paging services is also of concern, as it is expected that wireless offices will become a reality in the near future. Finally, the issue that never fails to crop up is security. Wireless LAN systems in general incorporate some form of security in transmissions, whether it is the use of data encryption techniques such as the data encryption standard (DES) or the use of spread-spectrum transmission, which has low detectability. A sensible quote to the idea of security in wireless LAN puts it, "It's beyond the abilities of most technically oriented users to tap into the spread-spectrum signala practical data thief would attack not the radio side of a network, but the cabled side" [7].

9.5 WIRELESS LAN DESIGN CONSIDERATIONS

In designing a wireless LAN system, several issues must be considered, such as the channel impairments, transmission techniques, and network architecture. In this section, we will briefly describe some of the design considerations on the air interface, channel coding, and network aspects.

One of the first issues in system design of wireless applications is the radio or air interface. The system must be robust to errors due to the fading and delay spreads of the channel, so it will require some form of channel coding to combat or reduce the effects of such transmission impairments. It is a well-known fact that the average attenuation slope of indoor radio propagation follows an exponent of 35–40 dB per decade (or a path loss exponent of 3.5 to 4) for the far field signal propagation and 20 dB per decade for the near field (which is close to free space). Due to the rapid signal decay indoors, the reuse factors will be low and may require more base stations strategically positioned to achieve ubiquitous coverage.

The choice of medium-access technologies will ultimately affect the capacity of the network, which is important in a wireless LAN. At present, there are two main techniques whereby access to the radio medium can be gained—time-division multiple access (TDMA) and code-division multiple access (CDMA). There are many different views about which technique is better, and going into detail will just confuse the whole issue.

The issue of delay spread will always be of concern due to its effect on wideband systems, such as CDMA or even TDMA, resulting in intersymbol interference (ISI). This may require the use of adaptive equalizers to balance the delays encountered in the radio channel. Equalization works by estimating the impulse response or transfer function of the transmission medium and constructing an inverse filter through which the received signal is passed. The use of this technique to combat delay spread impairments is discussed later in this chapter.

Because the radio channel is so unreliable in relaying information, due to the high error rates in the medium, considerations must be given to channel coding in the data stream. Efficient channel coding techniques must be chosen so that adequate error protection (FEC or ARQ) is implemented to ensure the integrity of data. The design of error-control techniques often requires the consideration of the applications and their tolerability to errors in order not to *overprotect* the data and introduce excessive overheads. Further details on error control was covered in Chapter 4.

All too often, attention is given to the design of the air interface rather than the network architecture. For the wireless LAN to be truly portable and live up to the expectations of mobile computing, emphasis must be given to the network design as well, so that full roaming between sites and networks can be supported as described in the previous chapter.

9.6 WIRELESS LAN TECHNOLOGIES AND SYSTEMS

Although wireless LAN systems are emerging [8–17], the market is still in its infancy. Currently, wireless LAN technologies comprise infrared (IR), UHF radio, spread spectrum, and microwave radio, ranging from frequencies in the region of 1.8 GHz in Europe (900 MHz in the U.S.) to infrared frequencies between 10^{14} and 10^{15} Hz. This section will describe some of the existing wireless LAN systems and enabling technologies. Table 9.1 summarizes the wireless LAN systems and technologies currently available in the U.S. and Europe.

9.6.1 Infrared Systems

The use of IR for data transmission is familiar to most households. One of the most popular applications for IR is in the remote control of TV sets, video cassette recorders, and stereo equipment. Over the past decade or so, IR technology has been reported for use in data transmission [18]. However, it is only recently that products are starting to emerge.

IR wireless LANs fall into two broad categories. The undirected technique is based on diffused radiation, and the point-to-point or directed transmission requires a line of sight (LOS).

Undirected IR techniques essentially use optical transceivers mounted near each station and aimed at a common spot (on the ceiling, for example), where a diffuser is located. IR rays arriving at this spot are then diffused to the surrounding environment, covering a range of 10m to 20m. A further example of a diffusive system is in [19], where the range has been extended up to a distance in excess of 30m indoors through the use of an effective optical concentrator, which provides an optical gain as compared to conventional isotropic emitters. Another undirected technique that does not require a LOS is the scattered IR system. Instead of directing at a diffuser, the transmitted rays bounce off walls and ceilings to reach nodes

TABLE 9.1

Summary of Existing Wirless LAN Systems

Company	Product	Data Rate	Frequency	Technology	LAN Topology	Features	Range
InfraLAN Technologies	InfraLAN	4/16 Mbps	Infrared	Infrared line-of-sight	Token ring	No license required	< 50m
Photonics	Infralink	40 Kbps	Infrared	Infrared scattered	Star	No license required	30–40m
California Microwave	Radiolink	250 Kbps	2.4 GHz	Frequency-hopping SS	Ethernet	No license required	200m
Telxon	ARLAN	1 Mbps	2.4 GHz	Direct-sequence SS	Ethernet	No license required; netware and TCP/IP support	80m
NCR	WaveLAN	2 Mbps	2.4 GHz	Direct-sequence SS	Ethernet	PCMCIA, Netware and LANtastic	250m
Olivetti	Netcubed (Net³)	1.152 Mbps	1.8 GHz	DECT-based UHF radio	Ethernet, token ring	CEPT-approved 1.8-GHz band data encryption	100m
Alps Electric	RadioPort	242 Kbps	ISM band	Spread spectrum	Ethernet	Netware and LANtastic	100–150m
Xircom	Netware	1 Mbps	2.4 GHz	Frequency-hopping SS	Ethernet, token ring	PCMCIA, parallel port, roaming, Netware, LANmanager	50m

TABLE 9.1 (continued)

Company	Product	Data Rate	Frequency	Technology	LAN Topology	Features	Range
Solectek	AirLAN	2 Mbps	ISM band	Direct-sequence SS	Ethernet	Netware, LANmanager, wireless bridge, and 64-bit DES	200–250m
Motorola	Altair II Plus	5.7 Mbps	18 GHz	Microwave TDMA	Ethernet	SNMP, TCP/IP, IPX, Vistapoint wireless bridge for point-to-point links	< 30m
Proxim	RangeLAN	242 Kbps	ISM band	Direct-sequence SS	Ethernet	Parallel port, PCMCIA connections, mobility support, roaming capabilities	100–150m
Proxim	RangeLAN 2	1.6 Mbps	ISM band	Frequency-hopping SS	Ethernet	PCMCIA and ISA connections, wireless bridge support, roaming capabilities	100–150m

within coverage. An example of a product using scattered undirected IR is the Infralink by Photonics. Performance is in the range of 40 Kbps, which is very limiting in most LAN applications. Although undirected systems do not require a LOS for transmission, they are limited in range (which is dependent on the reflectivity characteristics of the room) and not secure against eavesdroppers.

Directed IR techniques require a LOS between optical sensors in the transmitter and receivers. An example of such an implementation is the InfraLAN by InfraLAN Technologies [20].

The InfraLAN system is aimed at token-ring networks (IEEE 802.5), offering data throughput at 4 and 16 Mbps. The base station is a token-ring multistation access unit (MAU) with 6 medium interface connectors (MIC) used as ports for connection of token-ring workstations and devices. The base unit is also equipped with two ports for connecting an uplink and downlink optical node. Each optical node (operating at a wavelength of 850 nm) is an optical transceiver, capable of transmitting and receiving infrared signals. Electrical signals from the token-ring LAN are upconverted to IR light and transmitted by the optical node and then downconverted at the receiver to electrical token-ring signals again. For the simplest connection using the infraLAN system, two pairs of optical sensors (for upstream and downstream) with cables, two MAUs, and token-ring cables are required to achieve a server-to-workstation connection. A functional ring will therefore need six optical units and three MAUs.

The advantage of using infrared transmission is that it is unregulated and does not require a license. However although the system boasts of high-speed data transmission, the maximum distance between sensors is only 25m, due to the limitations of IR transmission. Indoors, the limiting noise source is light, such as fluorescent and incandescent lighting. The latter is more of a problem to IR because the spectral components of incandescent lighting fall within the region of IR. Fluorescent lighting, however, can be filtered out (by optical filtering) because its spectral components fall out of the band of interest. Sunlight can also be a problem if the transmitter or receiver is located near a window. This limits the signal coverage range of the transmitter and may fail to meet the needs of a portable system requiring the support of mobility.

9.6.2 Spread-Spectrum Wireless LANs

Spread-spectrum technology, originally developed for military communications due to its highly secure transmission properties, has recently stimulated commercial interest for wireless LANs and personal communications [21,22,23,24]. Commercial spread-spectrum products utilize the industrial, scientific, and medical (ISM) bands. In the U.S., these bands are located at 902–908 MHz, 2.4–2.4835 GHz, and 5.725–5.85 GHz [25]. In the U.K., an allocation of 2.445–2.475 GHz has been made available for spread-spectrum radio. Equipment is free to operate without a license in these frequency bands.

The principle behind spread-spectrum technology is that the radio signal at the transmitter is spread over a wide range of frequencies, making it difficult to intercept by unauthorized users. At the receiver, the signal is reconstructed back into its original form through a correlation process that filters out interference. Spread-spectrum radio appears in two forms, frequency hopping (FH) and direct sequence (DS) [21,22,26].

9.6.2.1   Frequency-Hopping Spread Spectrum

Frequency-hopping spread-spectrum systems (FHSS) hop from frequency to frequency within a specified band in a pseudorandom fashion. Transmitters and receivers will know a predetermined hopping sequence prior to transmission. FHSS is secure in that it is impossible to eavesdrop or jam a connection without advance knowledge of the hopping sequence and the dwell time between each frequency hop (time spent at each hop). Further, it mitigates multipath fading effects, as these tend to be frequency selective. However, FHSS requires precise frequency synchronization (i.e., fast frequency synthesizers) and therefore has high implementation costs. A typical FHSS system is shown in Figure 9.3.

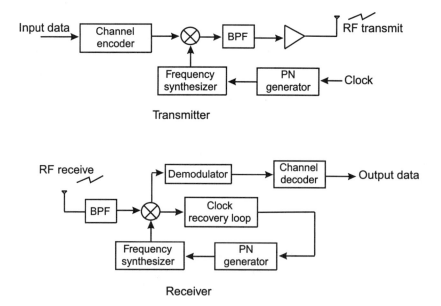

FIGURE 9.3 A typical frequency-hopping spread-spectrum system.

FH microwave transceivers developed by GEC Plessey Semiconductors perform data transmission at 704 Kbps. The chipset, which is integrated into a PCMCIA type II card, performs data management, hopping channel assignment, and radio control functions. The transceiver operates in the 2.4–2.483-GHz ISM band, with a double-superheterodyne receiver design. The extensive circuit integration is mounted on a 3 inch by 2 inch circuit board and is expected to find various applications in PDAs, wireless LANs, etc. [27,28].

A FHSS wireless LAN system is the RangeLAN2 [29], which is an enhancement to the original Product RangeLAN. The first-generation RangeLAN system was a direct-sequence spread-spectrum (DSSS) product in the 902–928-MHz ISM band; however, it permitted only 242-Kbps data throughput. The RangeLAN2 operates in the 2.4–2.483-GHz band and delivers an uncompressed data rate of 1.6 Mbps. The RangeLAN2 supports portable roaming capabilities, enabling microcellular architectures for in-building wireless LANs to be constructed. The coverage area supported by this system is between 100–150m in offices and up to 300m in open space.

Yet another FHSS wireless LAN system is that by Xircom. Known as the Netwave, Xircom's wireless LAN product provides radio coverage up to 50m, due to lower transmission power, so that the PCMCIA LAN adapter does not draw too much power. This extends the battery life of the portable PC. The adapter also takes advantage of the PC power-management system, powering down when the PC enters a sleep mode and powering up when operation resumes.

9.6.2.2 *Direct-Sequence Spread Spectrum*

With DSSS, each signal consists of a different pseudorandom binary sequence that modulates the carrier, spreading the spectrum of the waveform. A large number of DSSS signals may share the same frequency spectrum. If viewed in either the time or frequency domain, the multiple-access signals appear to be superimposed on top of each other. The signals are separated in the receivers by using a correlator, which accepts only signal energy from the selected binary sequence and despreads its spectrum. The other users' signals, whose codes do not match, are not despread in bandwidth and, as a result, contribute only to the noise. Figure 9.4 illustrates.

Data generated by the encoder/interleaver are multiplied by a spread code, which is often generated by the PN source at a much higher data rate. The number of spreading code bits is often called chips. Figure 9.5 illustrates the multiplication of the data stream by the spread code. The processing gain is the number of spreading code bits (chips) that fit in a data bit; in our example, the processing gain is four. The bandwidth required for the spread-spectrum signal is derived from the increase in signal bandwidth due to the processing gain. In Figure 9.5, the bandwidth required is four times the data rate.

The spreading code is unique to each wireless terminal and is used to spread and despread the data at the transmitter and receiver, respectively. This, therefore,

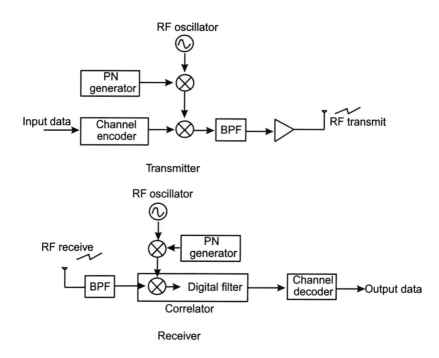

FIGURE 9.4 Direct-sequence spread spectrum and its principles.

allows many different users to share a common channel, hence *code division multiple access*. At the receiver, by multiplying the intended received spread-spectrum signal by the spread code, the original data can be recovered; other terminals utilizing the same channel will have a different spread code and the decorrelator will not be able to recover the transmitted data due to the different spread code. The output will appear as noise.

One of the first wireless LAN systems in the market is the ARLAN [30], which uses DSSS technology. Operating in the 2.4-GHz band, the ARLAN delivers a throughput of 1 Mbps. The ARLAN system also provides a range of products, including bridges.

Another DSSS wireless LAN system is the WaveLAN by NCR Corporation, which is very similar to the AirLAN by Solectek due to several cross-licensing agreements [29]. The WaveLAN has a chip rate of 11 Mchips per second, and this is used to spread the 2-Mbps signal offered into a wideband signal. The system provides relatively good coverage up to 300m from a transmit power of 250 mW. To boost its coverage area, NCR has a product called the WavePoint to extend the range of mobile users.

Although the range of the WaveLAN is good, it doesn't support roaming capabilities, as does RangeLAN, which is Proxim's first-generation DSSS product.

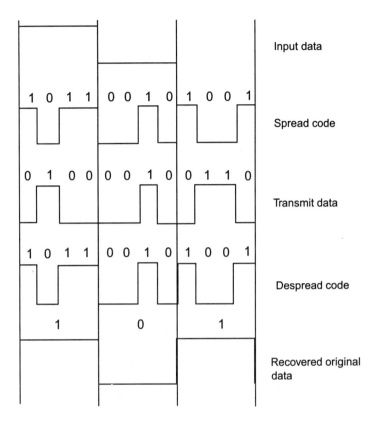

FIGURE 9.5 Spread-spectrum transmission.

Spread-spectrum wireless LANs have applications in various areas, such as airports, where a system with minimum interference to other airport radio systems is required. Other application areas include noisy manufacturing environments for the control of automatic guided vehicles (AGV) and the police force, where security is required.

9.6.3 UHF-Radio LANs

Although spread-spectrum wireless LAN systems utilize frequencies in the UHF band, we are considering it separately as a class on its own. In UHF-radio LAN systems, we look at DECT for the provision of a wireless LAN. As previously mentioned, DECT has been specified to support voice and data communications in the 1.88–1.9-GHz band in Europe. The data services supported include cordless access to LANs.

One of the problems associated with wireless LANs is the lack of standardization. Hence, the completion of the standard was welcomed as the first standard for wireless LANs. Although DECT supports a maximum data rate of 1.152 Mbps per carrier, only 768 Kbps is available for user data. An example of a DECT-based wireless LAN product is that by Olivetti Network Systems, known as the Netcubed or Net³. The DECT standard supports up to 250 mW and the coverage area ranges between 50m and 200m [31,32]. Although the bandwidth offered by DECT is not up to those offered by other spread-spectrum systems, DECT is rich in features supporting the mobility of wireless terminals, roaming capabilities, and integrated services. A brief description of a wireless LAN network based on DECT is discussed in Chapter 8 and in [33].

Although it may seem that DECT may not have the ability to offer data rates comparable to those advertised by spread-spectrum or IR systems, [34] showed quantitatively through computer simulations that DECT has the ability to support terminal login, e-mail, and file transfer protocol (for small files up to 20 KB) applications, even on a single 32-Kbps duplex time slot. With the current introduction of wireless PABXs in offices with CT2 technology offering 32 Kbps, the base stations could be further enhanced to support data connections. This could be done by using the wireless link to connect into existing LAN infrastructure to support applications such as TELNET and e-mail.

Higher bit-rate LAN applications using DECT multibearer connections have been simulated; these simulations are detailed in Chapter 8. A 256-Kbps LAN service can be supported on a connection involving 12 time slots in a carrier. Although limited in its ability to provide a high-bandwidth connection, DECT compensates by its wealth of features and flexibility in the integration of services.

9.6.4 Microwave Radio LANs

In this last category of wireless LANs, we have the microwave-radio LAN systems, operating at 18 GHz. Pioneered by Motorola, the product is known as the ALTAIR. The second-generation product, Altair II Plus [29] boasts a throughput of 5.7 Mbps, making it the highest performance wireless LAN system to date.

At 18 GHz, the signals are highly attenuated through multipath radio propagation, where signals are reflected/bounced off walls or people and arrive at the receiver at different phase angles, causing signal fading [35]. The signal transmission impairments caused by the radio propagation environment are detailed in Chapter 3. Because the signals can arrive at any direction and at any phase, the receiver must have omnidirectional coverage. To enable this, the ALTAIR uses a six-sectored intelligent antenna, where the transmitter and receiver negotiate the best signal path from 36 possible paths. This is determined from a table that is updated from the signal strengths monitored from each of the possible paths. This is explained in greater detail in [36]. The 25-mW, 18-GHz signal is highly attenuated in the indoor environment, limiting the coverage area to 30m, which explains the need for an advanced antenna system. Because of its limited range, Altair does not support mobility. In addition, microwave-device technology is still immature and LAN modules are bulky and heavy.

The network architecture is based on base stations or control modules (CM) attached to an existing Ethernet, which provides service to user modules (UM). UMs are typically single terminals. However, the UM and CM can be configured as a wireless LAN bridge when a UM attached to a LAN segment communicates with a CM attached on another LAN segment. The CM-UM link effectively functions as a bridge [37,38]. The CM is typically ceiling mounted, providing microcellular coverage with a radius of 40 ft, and is capable of supporting up to 32 workstations. Channel access is by time division multiplex access/time division duplex (TDMA/TDD), similar to the structure adopted by DECT.

Although it may seem advantageous to use the uncongested high-frequency bands for high bit-rate data transmission, the circuitry required is highly complex. ALTAIR uses gallium arsenide chips fabricated as monolithic microwave integrated circuits (MMIC) and high-speed digital signal processors (DSP) to achieve high-bit-rate transmissions with a six-sectored intelligent antenna system.

9.7 WIRELESS LAN INTERCONNECTION

From the use of wireless access into LANs, radio technology has been further exploited to support wireless internetworking, with wireless bridges linking remote segments of LANs, as illustrated in Figure 9.2. Wireless bridges provide connectivity to link LANs via radio rather than costly cables. An application scenario could be to link LANs in different buildings by means of wireless remote bridging [39]. Most of the wireless technologies as described in the previous section have products supporting wireless bridging—they appear with spread-spectrum technology, microwave, and laser. As with wireless LAN systems, the higher the frequency of operation, the higher the data rates that can be achieved—although the signal is more attenuated, so it covers a shorter range and requires LOS for communications.

Spread-spectrum wireless bridges operate in the ISM band offering maximum data rates of 2 Mbps. Solectek and Persoft have wireless bridges marketed under the names AirLAN bridge and Intersect, respectively. Motorola has enhanced its 18-GHz Altair LAN with the VistaPoint bridge. A unique system by Laser Communications offers the highest data rates for LAN bridging applications—they are comparable to fixed-wire speeds.

Another unique system that offers conventional wired data rates is the Digilink by Microwave Modules Ltd., which operates at 60.5 GHz. At this frequency, also known as the atmospheric absorption band, radio energy is absorbed by oxygen. This causes attenuation around 14 dB/km [40]. Because of this, the range is limited to less than 1 km. Such systems are typically roof-mounted outdoors, so they are affected by weather conditions such as rain or snow, which may reduce the range to 700m. However, Digilink supports 10-Mbps data transfer on any of its ten 10-MHz channels licensed in the U.K.

The relative throughputs of the bridges are dependent on the processing speed of the bridge. Every frame arriving at the bridge is similarly processed. When the frames are received, the header is examined and relayed to the destination LAN. Hence, the throughput is dependent on the speed that the headers are being processed. A data stream composing of a few large frames will require less processing than one made up of several small frames.

Therefore, one of the most effective methods to test the performance of a wireless bridge on an Ethernet is to send frames at 64 bytes (minimum packet size) and 1,518 bytes (maximum packet size) to check its frame-handling capabilities. The performance of the various wireless bridges [39] are summarized in Table 9.2.

TABLE 9.2

Summary of Wireless LAN Bridge Vendors and Their Performances
(*Source: Data Communications International*, McGraw Hill, Nov. 21, 1993, pp. 60–72.)

Vendor	Product	Data Rate per 64 Bytes	Data Rate per 1,518 Bytes	Frequency	Range	Network-Management Capabilities
Motorola	VistaPoint	442 Kbps	5.33 Mbps	18 GHz	up to 1.3 km	Yes (SNMP)
Solectek	AirLAN	373 Kbps	1.68 Mbps	ISM	Omni-directional: 150 m; 4-element YAGI: 2 km; 10-element YAGI: 6 km	No
Persoft	Intersect	940 Kbps	1.7 Mbps	ISM	Omni-directional: 200m; extendible to several km with directional antennas	Yes (SNMP)
Laser Communications	LCI L00-28	6.4 Mbps	9.5 Mbps	366 THz	1 km	No

9.8 STANDARDS FOR WIRELESS LANs

Although quite a few wireless LAN products are already on the market, the standards for wireless LANs are still in their infancy. The DECT standard is currently the only approved standard supporting wireless LAN applications [41]. It specifies the procedures for interworking between a DECT subnetwork with the International Standards Organization/International Electrotechnical Committee (ISO/IEC) 8802 LANs [42]. Based on this, DECT can be considered the world's first wireless LAN standard. The DECT standard is an air-interface standard, with the lower three layers (as compared to the OSI model) defined, supporting call management, mobility management, etc. Because it is a well-structured standard, integrated voice and data services can be supported, unlike other wireless LAN standards currently being developed, which have data only as an application. The DECT standard is strong in concept and technically sound with advanced handover features. It incorporates dynamic channel allocation techniques to increase the systems' capacities. The only drawback is that it has limited bandwidth for high-bit-rate LAN applications, although it will quite comfortably support terminal applications [34].

Other wireless LAN standardization efforts include the IEEE working group on wireless LANs, as part of the IEEE Project for LANs. The standard will be designated as the IEE 802.11 for wireless LANs. The project group aims to create a unified media access control (MAC) standard that will promote interoperability between wireless LAN equipment from various vendors. It will therefore allow IR LOS technology to coexist with spread spectrum and other LAN transmission types.

Various schemes were considered for the MAC protocol, including the reservation-based protocol, which uses a central control point to schedule transmissions. The transmitting station waits for the contention time of the protocol's constant-length frame and transmits a short request to send (RTS) message to the control point. The control point then notifies the station of its transmission time. Another consideration is the hybrid carrier sense multiple access with collision avoidance (CSMA/CA), which is a *listen before transmit* protocol based on a distributed control function. It is a variant of the CSMA/CD protocol used with conventional Ethernet LANs, with the enhancement of using RTS and clear to send (CTS) messages to avoid collisions. The messages inform stations within range of both the transmitting and receiving nodes that a data packet is about to be transmitted and to stay off the channel for a period of time. The latter CSMA/CA MAC protocol proposal was suggested by Xircom, NCR, and Symbol Technologies, and has been accepted by the IEEE 802.11 wireless LAN committee in standardizing the MAC layer.

The other considerations drafted by the IEEE 802.11 include independent network operation (companies sharing an office building should be able to operate their wireless networks without the need for coordination), security, power management, and internetworking.

The European Telecommunications Standards Institute (ETSI) standardization program for wireless LANs began in the early 1990s and can be categorized into three general categories offering various data rates. Table 9.3 details the different categories and their applications.

TABLE 9.3

ETSI Wireless LAN Standardization Categories

	Category 1	Category 2	Category 3
Data rate	250 Kbps	1–2 Mbps	15–20 Mbps
Technology	Spread spectrum	DECT	Under consideration
System density	1 Mbps/hectare/floor	3–10 Mbps/hectare/floor	100–1000 Mbps/hectare/floor
Applications	Standard terminals, office data communications	Advanced portable terminals, office networking	High-performance distributed computing
Frequency	2.4–2.5 GHz (ISM)	1.8–1.9 GHz	5.15–5.25 GHz 17.1–17.2 GHz

In addition to DECT, which supports voice and data communications, ETSI has set up working groups to develop the future of radio LANs in Europe. The Radio Equipment and Systems (RES) subtechnical committee, RES-10, will draft a standard for the high-performance European radio LAN (HIPERLAN). This standard, expected in 1995, will provide wireless data transmission at rates in the region of 15–20 Mbps.

The development of the HIPERLAN system requires the definition of a completely new air interface. Instead of developing a standard to achieve compatibility between existing wireless LAN systems, the aim was to create a robust air-interface supporting 20-Mbps data transmission. However, at such a specification in the indoor radio propagation channel, problems such as ISI will be present. In order to overcome this, various techniques to combat ISI were considered, such as adaptive equalization, multicarrier modulation schemes, and use of antennas with diversity and directivity [43].

With adaptive equalization, ISI can be eliminated. An adaptive equalizer requires training and tracking. A known training sequence is first transmitted, which is then used at the receiver (by utilizing an algorithm) to estimate the impulse response of the channel. Based on this, proper filter coefficients are adjusted for in the equalizer. After training, real data is sent and the equalizer tracks the variations in the channel in a decision-directed mode. For the indoor radio channel, the latter process is often not required, due to the slowly varying nature of the channel.

Another technique considered in the development of high-bit-rate LAN without ISI is the use of multicarrier modulation, which is effective in overcoming radio propagation delay spreads. By dividing a wideband channel such as the HIPERLAN channel into a number of narrowband subchannels, each using a subchannel carrier (hence "multicarrier"), the wideband frequency-selective fading channel is effectively transformed into a number of flat fading channels. Because frequency-selective fading is experienced when the bandwidth of transmission is greater than the coherence bandwidth of the channel (which is inversely proportional to the channel delay spread), the problem can be overcome by using a number of narrowband channels.

The use of such techniques for the HIPERLAN has both pros and cons. With multicarrier modulation, both of the RF power amplifiers and the receiver front ends must be linear to limit intermodulation distortion (IMD) products. With adaptive equalization techniques, baseband processing requirements are high and computation complexity may surpass the ability of current DSP technology and may require innovative implementation techniques.

9.9 THE FUTURE OF THE WIRELESS LAN

The developments in the wireless LAN industry implies exciting times for the future of portable and mobile computing. Portable computer terminals will be able to access network services ubiquitously. Computing will no longer be bound to cables and will be able to roam not only in the local network, but also in the private and foreign networks. The wireless workplace will become a reality. With high-performance LAN standards emerging, outperforming conventional existing wired LANs, a new wave of applications will be introduced, such as wireless multimedia and videoconferencing. Indeed, there is a lot to expect in the future of mobile data with wireless LANs.

References

[1]   Libbenga, J., "When Worlds Collide," *Mobile Europe*, Vol. 3, No. 1, Jan. 1993, pp. 22–23.

[2]   Freeburg, T.A., "Enabling Technologies for Wireless In-Building Network," *IEEE Communications Magazine*, Vol. 29, No. 4, April 1991, pp. 58–64.

[3]   Murphy, K.C., "Directions in Mobile Computing," *Electronic Design*, Nov. 22, 1993, pp. 101.

[4]   Leonard, M., "Communication Terminals Get Personal," *Electronic Design*, Feb. 4, 1993, pp. 61–67.

[5]   IEEE 802.11, "Wireless LAN Requirements," Document IEEE 802.11/91-108.

[6]   Rappaport, T.S., "Indoor Radio Communications for Factories of the Future," *IEEE Communications Magazine*, May 1989, pp. 15–23.

[7]   Anderson, D., and J. Molyneaux, "Three Technical Hurdles on the Road to a Wireless Office—Integration, Integration, Integration," *Proc. IEEE Conference on Selected Topics of Wireless Communications*, 1992, pp. 387–390.

[8] Hallinan, C., "Cableless LANs: The Network of the Future?" *Telecommunications*, Vol. 25, No. 6, June 1991, pp. 51–55.

[9] Brown, R., "The Wireless Office Untethers Networks," *Networking Management*, Vol. 10, No. 7, June 1992, pp. 42–45.

[10] Brodsky, I., "Cordless LANs Hits the Airwaves," *Telecommunications*, Vol. 25, No. 9, September 1991, pp. 119, 150.

[11] Whitehouse, B., "Cableless Connections," *Network*, November 1990, pp. 87–95.

[12] King, J., "LANs on the Loose," *Network*, November 1992, pp. 59–66.

[13] Shandle, J., "No Strings Attached," *Electronics*, March 1991, pp. 29, 45–48.

[14] Special issue on "Wireless Indoor Communications," *IEEE Network Magazine*, Vol. 5, No. 6, November 1991.

[15] Tuttlebee, W., *Cordless Telecommunications In Europe*, London: Springer-Verlag, 1991.

[16] Young, K., "Cut the Cable," *Communications Networks*, April 1992, pp. 39–42.

[17] Shetty, V., "The Wireless Workplace," *Communications International*, Nov. 92, pp. 89–90.

[18] Gfeller, F.R., and U.R. Bapst, "Wireless In House Data Communications via Diffuse Infra-red Radiation," *Proceedings IEEE*, Vol. 67, No. 11, Nov. 1979, pp. 1474–1486.

[19] Pauluzzi, D.R., P.R.H. McConnell, and R.L. Poulin, "Free-Space, Undirected Infra-red (IR) Voice and Data Communications with a Comparison to RF Systems," *Proceedings IEEE Conference on Selected Topics in Wireless Communications*, ICWC '92, 1992, pp. 279–285.

[20] *LAN Times*, Vol. 10, No. 14, New York: McGraw Hill, July 26, 1993, pp. 90–92.

[21] Taub, H., and D.L. Schilling, "Principles of Communications Systems," Second Edition, New York: McGraw Hill, 1980.

[22] Sklar, B., *Digital Communications*, Englewood Cliffs, NJ: Prentice Hall, 1988.

[23] Special Issue on "Personal Communications," *IEEE Communications Magazine*, Vol. 29, No. 2, February 1991.

[24] Special Issue on "Personal Communications Systems," *IEEE Communications Magazine*, Vol. 30, No. 12, December 1992.

[25] Schilling et al., "Spread Spectrum for Commercial Communications," *IEEE Communications Magazine*, Vol. 29, No. 4, April 1991.

[26] Walters, L.C., "Shannon Coding and Spread Spectrum, Parts 1 to 4," *Electronics and Wireless World*, Jan., March, April, May, 1989

[27] Electronic Product Design, "An Integrated Microwave Transceiver," London, May 1993, pp. 33–34

[28] Leonard, M., "PCMCIA-sized Radio Links Portable Wireless LAN Terminals," *Electronic Design*, Aug. 5, 1993, pp. 45–50

[29] Capen, T., "Cutting the Cord," *Infoworld*, Vol. 15, No. 40, Oct. 4, 1993, pp. 95–97.

[30] Zenko, W., "Breakthrough in Radio Technology Offers New Application Options," *Proc. IEEE Vehicular Navigation and Information Systems Conference*, 1989, pp. 384–388.

[31] Davies, W., "Wireless LANs—Some User Concerns," *Telecommunications News*, p. 7, 1991.

[32] van der Hoek, Hans, "The New DECT Standard for Cordless Communications," *Telecommunications*, February 1993, pp. 77–80.

[33] Wong, P., "Mobile Computing in a LAN Environment," *Proceedings IEEE ICC 94*, New Orleans, May 1–5, 1994.

[34] Wong, P., and F. Halsall, "Data Applications for DECT," *Proc. IEEE International Conference on Communications*, Geneva, Switzerland, May 23–26, 1993, pp. 49.5.1–5.

[35] Mitzlaf, J., "Radio Propagation and Anti Multipath Techniques in the WIN," *IEEE Network Magazine*, Vol. 5, No. 6, November 1991, pp. 21–26.

[36] Bucholz, D., P. Odlyzko, M. Taylor, and R. White, "Wireless In-building Network Architecture and Protocols," Vol. 5, No. 6, *IEEE Network*, November 1991, pp. 31–38 .

[37] Halsall, F., *Data Communications, Computer Networks and Open Systems*, Third Edition, Reading, MA: Addison Wesley, 1992.

[38] Stallings, W., *Data and Computer Communications*, Third Edition, New York: Maxwell Macmillan, 1991.

[39] Tolly, K., and D. Newman, "Wireless Internetworking," *Data Communications Magazine*, McGraw-Hill, Nov. 21, 1993, pp. 60–72.

[40] MacLeod, A., "Pipe in the Sky Avoids Digging Up Roads," *New Electronics on Campus*, Autumn 1993, pp. 6–7.

[41] Hayes, V., "Standardization Efforts for Wireless LANs," *IEEE Network Magazine*, Vol. 5, No. 6, November 1991.

[42] ETSI, "DECT System Description Document," ETSI Draft European Technical Report Version 3.4, DR/RES 3004, Valbonne, France, June 1992.

[43] Li, M. et al, "Study of Air Interface Techniques for Wireless LANs," *Proceedings IEE Colloquium on the Cordless Office*, Digest 1993/172, London, Oct. 5, 1993, pp. 4/1–7.

CHAPTER 10
▼▼▼

MOBILE DATA APPLICATIONS

Mobile data has progressed slowly from being an *add on* to mobile radio voice systems to become a specific market of its own. In the early days, the markets were what are now described as vertical, which in marketeer speak means that they are related to a particular user or industry that has a specific need for mobile data. A bus company that uses the data channel for the transmission of location information about its vehicles is a good example. As a technology or application matures it tends to become horizontal, which means that the application crosses the boundaries of user type. A good example of this is e-mail, where messages are sent and received between diverse users. The content of these messages is general and need not have a direct functional bearing on the industries concerned.

Until now, major applications for mobile data have all been in the vertical market segment. However, new ones are gradually shifting to the horizontal segment, as data services over analog and digital cellular, public data networks, and wireless LANS (such as DECT) allow more general interconnection between diverse users.

10.1 MOBILE DATA HORIZONTAL FUNCTIONS

The main horizontal functions of mobile data usage can be broken down into four categories:

- Dispatch;
- Database inquiry and update;

- Interpersonal messaging (e-mail and paging);
- Remote control/reporting.

Dispatch is perhaps the most well-known use of mobile data, where a courier or taxi company is given a job assignment or an address. This particular application verges on the vertical, as it is an essential part of the working methodology but it is used by several industries, particularly the utilities, where it has been in service for several decades.

Database inquiry covers an even broader field. An example of this is when a service engineer has been dispatched to a job and needs to order or verify that spares are available, or to remotely access an electronic service manual. Motor insurance assessors can access price lists of replacement car parts and generate an estimate on the spot. Firemen can access hazardous chemical databases to check the correct means of tackling an incident—using the wrong foam on a chemical fire could have disastrous results. Policemen can check the stolen-vehicles register if they become suspicious and believe that a vehicle is either stolen or is carrying the wrong license plates. Retailers can check the validity of credit cards and make debit card transactions.

The simplest form of messaging is paging, which is a one-way service. In increasing complexity the next level is acknowledgment paging, through to the higher level of e-mail, and finally to electronic data interchange (EDI).

Finally, remote control and reporting has several variants. Telemetry is very often one-way but requires a two-way data function for verification and data checking. This can be either remote outstations reporting into a control center or, conversely, a control center sending messages out to control road signs on highways. Big users of remote wireless telemetry are the water and gas utilities which, unlike the electricity suppliers, have no copper wires to transport their signaling. Cable-borne carrier systems are used by many electricity suppliers to carry voice and data but, in an increasing number of cases, fiber-optic filaments are buried in or wrapped around the cables, which give greatly increased data capacities.

10.2   EXAMPLES OF VERTICAL APPLICATIONS

Depending on the levels of mobility, applications vary between the use of inhouse wireless LANs, which are used for computer networking purposes, to field activities, which can involve long distance communications via satellites. Most classic mobile data applications are associated with data from terminals fitted in vehicles. They transmit over the standard private mobile radio (PMR) frequency allocations in the VHF and UHF bands. Many of the earlier applications were involved with vehicle tracking or automatic vehicle location (AVL), as it is generically known. By their very nature, private data networks have been vertically oriented, and it is worthwhile to look at some of the successful implementations.

Security companies have a need to track their vehicles, particularly when carrying high-value cargos, so that they can be easily traced if they are hijacked. Applications have used map following, dead reckoning, and distance traveled, supplemented by wayside beacons to update the onboard computers to determine the vehicle position. Later LORAN C and Decca Navigator were used for some land-based applications. Most current system designs have concentrated on the use of global positioning system (GPS) satellites to determine location, but even this has to be supplemented by some other navigation scheme in dense urban areas and tunnels, where the satellites cannot be "seen." Dead reckoning, most commonly used tracking method in this situation, relies on the vehicle's odometer to measure distance traveled and a gyro compass to estimate the direction of travel. Alternatives to GPS include DataTrack, which uses low-frequency radio beacons installed across the country, and an interesting scheme based on radio interferometry called Cursor, which uses the carrier of local broadcast radio stations. The receivers for this latter system require very narrow filters to remove the modulation, and this may cause problems at high speeds due to Doppler shift.

Bus companies have used AVL for some time, not only to keep track of where the buses are but to enable rescheduling and to supply information to passengers waiting at stops on how long it will be before the next bus will arrive. In Ireland, Dublin Bus has been running such a scheme for over 15 years. Some 1,500 buses are polled in sequence to send back location and load data. The data rate is 2.4 Kbps and uses subcarrier modulation in a 25-kHz separated channel. This scheme requires only the use of the odometer to measure the distance traveled, as it is unusual for a bus to stray from its allotted route. The odometer is reset to zero at the start of each journey and a worse-case error was found to be less than 300 m over route lengths of several kilometres. In the event of bus bunching, it was found possible to persuade passengers to leave one bus and join another to make up a full load on one bus and reschedule the other. This resulted in more efficient running of the buses, fewer delays, and greater passenger satisfaction because the service could be relied upon. Average journey times were also reduced. It is interesting to note that the buses are polled. Polling allows the greatest use of the available radio channel resource, where usage of each of the two frequencies (uplink and downlink) is approaching one erlang. No voice communication is allowed on the data channel, and a speech request is made in the polled status message. If the request is accepted, the controller sends a message to command the vehicle to go to a separate channel for the conversation. The only exception is an emergency call which can pre-empt a polling cycle. Polling is the most efficient of the access methods if all units require regular access to the system. However, in the majority of cases, random access is achieved by the methods outlined in Chapter 7, where different network operators have chosen different methods based on the type of predicted traffic. In the analog trunking access standard MPT 1327 [1] it is interesting to note that, although the basic access method is variable-length slotted aloha, provision has been made to migrate to polling groups in order to maintain system stability if the control channel becomes overloaded.

A novel variation of the normal dispatcher operation has been introduced by one of the London taxi cab cooperatives. In a small dispatch operation with a few tens of vehicles, the controller is able to maintain knowledge of the cabs' status and their approximate position, and has little difficulty with job allocations. In a system with one to two thousand vehicles on the street at the same time and under the control of up to four dispatchers, it is very difficult—without the use of sophisticated computer control—to be aware of the exact situation at any one time. A very simple means of offering jobs to drivers has been devised based on the random-access protocol inherent in the data system. If a customer phones the cab company for a pickup, the dispatcher broadcasts a bid request to all cabs together with the pickup location. Those free within a defined radius of, say, a quarter of a mile may make a bid if they wish by pressing one of the status buttons. The random-access protocol sorts out the call clashes, and the unit that answers the call first is automatically awarded the job.

Rail companies are making greater use of wireless data than ever before. In the past, any use of radio, whether for speech or data, had to be backed up by more conventional signaling means on the grounds of safety. The railway industry is one of the most conservative in the safety field. Until recently, some companies even refused the use of error correction on the grounds that there was a chance that a false correction could occur and a dangerous situation could develop. It has taken considerable persuasion to show that error correction in association with separate error detection yields no worse falsing than error detection on its own. The new Jubilee line extension of the London Underground subway system will feature data over radio as the means for train control although initially, and maybe always, there will be a driver present to take over if necessary.

Other major users of data in the transportation field include American Courier and Federal Express, which use simple dispatch systems and acknowledgment messaging with their drivers to confirm acceptance of jobs. Significant improvements in productivity have resulted from the introduction of mobile data.

Glab (Göteborgsregionens Lokaltrafik AB) is a major public transport company based in Sweden, which operates a fairly sophisticated mobile data network. It has around 400 vehicles equipped with information and positioning systems to provide data to the bus operators and to bus stops. Glab itself does not run the buses or trams but employs traffic providers from competing bus, tram, train, ferry, and taxi companies to whom it supplies the data services. Mobitex equipment has been progressively installed in the vehicles since 1989, and now all of the vehicles have terminals. It is the company's intention to improve the public transportation services enough to reduce the use of private vehicles by at least 10% by the end of the century. Voice is still regarded as an essential part of this system to enable the drivers access to the PSTN. One of the services offered is that of integrated, nonscheduled transport, where a passenger may ask the driver to arrange a taxi pickup at a particular bus stop in order to complete his journey. At this time, the easiest way of doing this is to use speech, but in time this too may be integrated in the data system.

Police forces throughout the world are looking at the use of mobile data very seriously, as it offers many advantages over voice systems in the ease of encryption, the security, and the accuracy of the data transmitted. Motorola have supplied several of these systems in the U.S. and Europe. The main use to which they are put is database inquiries, which include license-plate checks on vehicles to see if they are stolen, wanted-person inquiries, stolen property inquiries, and even criminal-record checks. The latter has caused concern with civil liberties groups because of the open nature of the radio channel and the possibility of interception by unauthorized parties. It can be shown that even a modest level of scrambling is more than sufficient to allay these fears—only the most sophisticated of criminals would have the resources to break the codes.

The utilities have been at the forefront in the use of mobile data, as they tend to have a large mobile workforce engaged in service activities. A particularly successful implementation has been made made by Washington Gas in Virginia, which supplies gas to an area of 2,500 square miles. The company has a maintenance staff of 300, all of whom have been equipped with Motorola KDT units on a dedicated Ardis-like system (because the Ardis network itself gave insufficient coverage in the more remote areas).The cost of the system has been of the order of $3 million, but this outlay is expected to be recouped in less than three years by improved productivity. The main benefit has been the increased number of service calls possible with the same level of staffing because the maintenance staff is able to operate from home without going into the office each day to pick up work schedules. Unfortunately, due to union pressure and other tax issues concerning the length of the work day, this method of working has had to be suspended. Technology alone is unable to improve efficiency if the will is not there. Even so, other benefits that are more difficult to quantify have emerged. The system has improved the overall service to the extent that Washington Gas are planning additional enhancements, which will include the introduction of pen-based laptop computers and bar code scanners for spare parts.

Many other networks that have not yet migrated from vertical to general-purpose use exist, such as existing AVL systems used in public transportation and the automobile rescue associations in the U.K., North America, and Australia, where the data systems have been installed for the specific purposes of providing secure communication and supplementing the voice system.

10.3 ARDIS

The Ardis network is a classic case of two private networks that amalgamated and evolved into a public access network. The two private networks were owned by IBM and Motorola, respectively. The IBM network had been set up in the early

1980s to provide IBM's service engineers with a means of obtaining information from a central database while on a customer's premises. This added a constraint on the RF-system design to provide good in-building coverage in the areas where potential and existing customers resided. This resulted in the base stations being sited in the business districts of the major cities. Motorola's system was smaller but gave good coverage in New York, Chicago, and Los Angeles—the three major business cities in the U.S. With the amalgamation, the resultant network covers 400 metropolitan areas with some 1,300 base stations. It is claimed that the network covers 80% of the population and as much as 90% of business locations.

Since the formation of the joint venture in 1990, combining the system integrator skills of IBM and the radio expertise of Motorola, what started out as a very specific vertical application for both companies has now migrated to the provision of services to many other users via airtime agreements. The network now has some 60 customers, who operate some 30,000 mobile units. Gradually the technology is being upgraded to allow for the increase in traffic from the original 4.8-Kbps single channel scheme (the same frequency was reused across the U.S.) through the use of RD-LAP (see Chapter 7) at 19.2 Kps in a 25-kHz channel. (In Europe, this is restricted to 9.6 Kbps, as up to now only 12.5-kHz channels have been allocated for mobile data.) Most customers will be unaware of the increase in the speed of the data, except where it affects the grade of service, as messages are generally short and the delays introduced come from host computer processing times and transit times across the fixed-packet infrastructure.

Ardis's strategy continues to concentrate on providing its customers with vertical market applications. These include field services as before for Motorola and IBM, but new customers such as the service staff of the OTIS elevator company, parking enforcement in the public sector, and home insurance sales are using the network. In addition, United Parcel Service is a major transportation customer.

Recently it was announced that Motorola bought out IBM's share of the network and will run it as a separate business entity. This is just one example of the development of a mobile data network that started as a specific user requirement.

10.4 DATA ON PUBLIC ACCESS MOBILE RADIO NETWORKS

Over the last few years, and particularly in Sweden, taxi companies have been migrating to mobile data. Initially, dispatcher voice systems were overlaid with a data capability that allowed a driver to bid for a job issued by the dispatcher. Now the system allows the receipt of printed instructions such as pickup addresses and account client details. Even credit-card validation is becoming commonplace, but this again introduces the problem of security, and it is necessary to include a level of encryption on the network or within the application. Many of the smaller companies are unable to afford the cost of their own data system, so they have subscribed in increasing numbers to the public data networks. Although these networks provide *transparent transport* of the data, the end user is very often not in a position to provide his own application. A new business of *system integrators* or *application providers* is springing up. British Airways' Speedwing Mobile Communications company has provided its parent with mobile data applications, including the remote checking in of passengers, which greatly alleviates the crowds at the check-in desks, and the provision of bidirectional passenger and aircraft load and fuel data for the aircraft loading teams. With this experience, they offer other potential users a service to generate application interfaces to order. In particular, they wish to capitalize on their existing applications and persuade other airlines to use them.

Many other companies, such as Hewlett Packard, DEC and IBM, have the in-house expertise to generate their own application packages, but many others require help from specialist companies. In the case of the Glab transport system, a small software company called Hogia Communications has been responsible for writing all of the code, in close cooperation with the managers in the bus companies. Hogia is not a very large company; it has about 130 staff members worldwide, with the majority in Sweden. This setup is fairly typical of the type of company involved with this sort of work, as it is necessary to be extremely flexible and to be able to immerse the application writers in the day-to-day running of the company for whom the application is being written. The position of the systems integrator is crucial to the success of this segment of the market.

Recently, several of the major software suppliers have been adapting existing LAN-based e-mail solutions to interface with the major data networks, which include RAM, Ardis (Data TAC), and CDPD. Various strategic alliances have been forged. Apple has an agreement with France Telecom for data over CT2 (Beebop) in Paris. Lotus and Novell are providing products to RAM, as are the Digital Equipment Corporation (DEC). Microsoft is developing software products that will operate over various mobile data networks, as well as the analog and digital cellular networks.

Wireless e-mail is seen by many as the mass-market horizontal product offering, and all of the major software houses have produced their versions. Another product that shows promise is mobile facsimile. The message is sent over the data network in character form to a fax server gateway, where it is encoded and then sent over the PSTN. This service is one way from mobile to fax receiver, but has great advantages due to the number of terminals that can be accessed. Many smaller companies do not have e-mail connection, particularly in Europe, but the vast majority do have a fax machine.

The majority of the users connected to the mobile data networks are still located in the vertical market segment and operate their own specific applications. The main reason these users are connected to the public networks is that they need larger coverage than can economically be justified with an individual network. There is also no necessity for them to apply for their own frequencies or license.

International roaming in Europe is now becoming an issue with long-distance ruckers (and business people) who wish to maintain data communication on their travels and who require ubiquitous coverage. The GSM cellular network is capable of this, but the associated costs are very high. Mobitex is available in many of the western European countries, the U.S., and Canada, and offers a potentially international service. The DataTAC system is being introduced into Australia and several Southeast Asian countries, and should be able to offer a similar service there.

One of the biggest barriers to the universal use of mobile data has been the cost of the hardware. The price of the radio modems has been higher than the average consumer can tolerate or is accustomed to, with the purchase price of subsidized cellular phones. Several manufacturers are developing PCMCIA card modems and modem interfaces, where large levels of integration and numbers should bring the manufacturing costs down. Most public data networks are unable to subsidize the cost of user terminal equipment because call charges have to be highly competitive to maintain competitiveness with the cellular networks, and margins are therefore lower. With the advent of greater standardization of transmission methods and frequency allocations, such as the introduction of the TETRA packet data optimized standard in 1995, it is hoped that terminal equipment will become more competitively priced due to the increased production volumes that should ensue. However, at the same time, increased competition will come from the data services offered on the cellular networks, particularly from the second-generation digital ones and from CDPD. Many of the systems integrators are writing their applications in such a way that they are not network-specific, or, if they are, they can be changed with the minimum of effort so that it is immaterial which technology is used. All of which indicates that mobile data is about to take off!

References

[1] MPT 1327 "A Signalling Standard for Trunked Private Land Mobile Radio Systems," Radiocommunications Agency, London, first published 1988, reprinted and revised November 1991.

CHAPTER 11
▼▼▼

THE FUTURE OF MOBILE DATA COMMUNICATIONS

The mobile data market is set to explode in the latter part of this decade. It is expected that mobile data will be a mass-market service offering personal communications services that will support a wide range of applications for every user. In this chapter, we will look at future systems and applications, and networks that we can expect in the near future.

11.1 PERSONAL DIGITAL ASSISTANTS—A VEHICLE FOR MOBILE DATA

Currently, one of the most promising future portable computing markets is the personal digital assistant (PDA)—also known as personal information managers (PIM). These are advanced electronic organizers with capabilities that include scheduling and pen-based input incorporating handwriting recognition. These palmtop computers will usher in a new era of personal portable computing. The first generation of PDAs are already in existence, among them are the Apple Newton, the Amstrad Pen Pad, the AT&T EO Personal Communicator, and the Tandy (Casio) Zoomer. These devices combine pen input, handwriting recognition, personal organization tools (such as taking notes, keeping a diary, and scheduling appointments), and sending and receiving faxes and e-mail messages. In the future, we should expect to see further capabilities such as video telephony and wireless access to LANs, corporate and personal databases, and the ability to perform electronic transactions such as banking, shopping, and travel reservations. These devices will be a vehicle to catapult mobile data communications to the mass market. Already, France Telecom is developing an interface between its CT2 Telepoint service and PDAs [1].

One of the most advanced first-generation PDAs on the market is the AT&T EO 440 and 880 Personal Communicator. Highly integrated, this "Rolls Royce" of PDAs combine fax, e-mail, wireless (cellular) voice, data access, and pen-based computing into one single unit. In addition, communication with other devices is possible over various interfaces, such as a serial port for data transfer between the PDA and any IBM-compatible PC; a parallel port for connection to printers, LANs (via parallel port adapters), and floppy disk drives; a keyboard port for heavy data entries with PC-compatible keyboards; Type II PCMCIA slots for expansion and connectivity via PCMCIA-based wireless modems; and an RJ-11 port to connect to standard telephone lines. This is an integration feat by today's standards and offers enormous flexibility to users.

PCMCIA slots are currently a de facto standard in portable computers. Most notebook computers have at least one slot for connection with LANs, fixed wire modems, wireless modems, etc. As a result, wireless LAN cards are now manufactured in the PCMCIA format. In the near future, we should expect to see most wireless data modems manufactured in this format to enable portable connectivity. PDAs and portable computers with the PCMCIA slots are then able to plug into wireless modems to gain access to the fixed network, wherever they may roam. Such modems will conform to the various air-interface standards—for example GSM, IS-54 DECT, or CDPD—and by changing the modems, PDAs will be able to connect to the appropriate network.

In the future, we also expect to see intelligent multimode terminals serving access to a variety of networks and systems [2,3]. Using reprogrammable digital signal processors and frequency synthesizers to implement programmable multisystem terminals, support for different networks can be implemented via software and modular RF interfaces.

11.2   FUTURE MOBILE DATA SERVICES

Among the most talked about of future mobile data services is the portable video telephone. This will be a terminal that supports wireless and portable two-way video telephony. With the current rate of advancement in image compression technology [4,5], the vision of such a future service supporting multimedia applications will not be far away. In Europe, under the Research for Advanced Communications in Europe (RACE) program, a project on the development of a mobile audio visual terminal (MAVT) [6] has been undertaken to develop algorithms for low-bit-rate video ($p \times 8$ Kbps), audio coding for portable video terminals, terminal design, and channel coding.

Portable video terminals of the future are expected to be highly portable and permit easy access to commercial information databases. Video databases can be made available on demand, giving users the freedom to access video information as required. Video terminals can further be extended to provide two-way end-to-end video telephony, as well as store-and-forward video mail services if the end user is unable to be contacted. Such terminals can also be used for teleshopping applications, as well as reception of TV or satellite broadcasts. With device integration, video coding, and digital radio techniques, we may be able see such portable terminals even before the turn of the century.

In addition, mobile data communications have also found applications in road transport informatics to improve efficiency, safety, and convenience of traveling with vehicle navigation systems. More commonly known as intelligent-vehicle highway systems or intelligent transportation systems, these vehicle-navigation systems provide vehicle location on an electronic map, route optimization, and real-time traffic updating, based on broadcast traffic and travel information. Such systems use comprehensive road-system databases (digital maps) stored on CD-ROMs. Together with satellite global positioning systems (GPS) such as NAVSTAR [7], electronic compasses, wheel sensors, and roadside beacons (broadcasting up-to-date travel information), the navigation computer is able to calculate the optimum route based on distance or shortest-time requirements. In addition to vehicle navigation, other applications include automatic debiting, toll management, and parking lot management. They are further detailed in [8].

11.3 INTEGRATION OF SECOND-GENERATION DIGITAL SYSTEMS

Second generation wireless network systems such as GSM, DECT, and ERMES (ERMES is an acronym for European messaging system, which is a pan-European digital paging standard) are currently being actively deployed in Europe. Before the next-generation systems offering personal communications start to appear, we should expect to see these systems interworking with one another, to provide ubiquitous wireless personal communications. Both DECT and GSM have been defined with interoperability in mind, with DECT being used primarily for indoor local-coverage communications and GSM being used for outdoor wide-area communications.

Take the following scenario for example. A senior executive at a London-based company leaves his office to fly to a corporate meeting in Brussels. As he walks to his car, a call comes in for him and is immediately routed to his DECT handset via the nearest base station of his office cordless PBX. In his car he has a GSM phone with a DECT base station with interworking capabilities. As the call carries on, he drives off, still using his DECT handset via the DECT base station interworking with the GSM car phone. The call is continued transparently via the GSM network.

At the same time, another corporate executive from Paris starts to make his way to Brussels for the same meeting. As he waits for his flight at the airport, he makes a call to a friend based in Milan using his DECT handset via a telepoint. The friend is on a business trip to Stockholm. The call gets to the friend's direct line in Milan. Meanwhile in Stockholm, upon arrival, the company asks if the Italian visitor has a DECT handset to register with the cordless PBX so that he can receive incoming calls. Upon registration, his new location is updated and his home PBX in Milan is also updated. The call from Paris to Milan is then routed to Stockholm. So even when he is away from his office, he can still be reached. While waiting for his flight, the executive wishes to update his report based on developments earlier that morning. With his portable computer, capable of DECT wireless access via the telepoint, he is able to access any files he wishes from his office.

At the corporate meeting in Brussels, the executives register their handsets and portable computers with the base stations at the corporate headquarters. The base stations are also attached to the LAN so that executives are able to access computer databases and e-mail back at their home offices. Before the meeting starts one of the executives retrieves a file containing a report that he intends to distribute at the meeting via the DECT wireless LAN. When the transfer is finished, he then prints out the file via the local printer. Hence, he need not carry copies of reports/spread sheets to meetings, enabling him to travel lighter. At the same time during the meeting, his colleague realizes that he has forgotten some figures for his presentation. Using his DECT wireless LAN connection, he accesses a report with the appropriate figures and presents it at the meeting. At the end of the meeting, all of the information exchanged and discussed can then be relayed back to the respective offices via the network.

At the end of the meeting, the secretary relays the conclusions of the meeting to an executive on vacation in a remote countryside resort in Spain. The minutes of the meeting are electronically mailed and faxed to him because his GSM car phone is out of range. A paging message can be sent via the ERMES paging network to inform him that the fax is waiting for him. On his way back, as soon as he gets within the GSM coverage, he turns on his GSM fax machine, which prints out the fax message stored in the fax mail. In addition, he could also use the GSM network to check his e-mail account for any messages sent to him during his vacation.

With all the three systems interworking with one another, PCS can be achieved from one end of Europe to the other, from DECT telepoints to GSM networks to ERMES and to DECT wireless LANs, information can always be relayed or retrieved wherever one is.

11.4 EVOLUTION OF THIRD-GENERATION NETWORKS

Many first-generation systems—TACS, AMPS, and CT1—were originally developed without any consideration to mobile data transmission. However, second-generation wireless networks, such as GSM, DECT, TETRA, DSRR, American Digital Cellular (ADC), and Japanese Digital Cellular (JDC) have data transmission capabilities purposely designed into the system, allowing for low (up to 19.2 Kbps) to medium data transmission rates (up to 1 Mbps). While these systems support data communications, they are limited, due to incompatibility between the systems. Future wireless networks will therefore attempt to break down this barrier and unite all of the different systems into one, supporting global interworking and roaming abilities. Three very ambitious projects—the Future Public Land Mobile Telecommunications System (FPLMTS), the Universal Mobile Telecommunications System (UMTS), and the Universal Personal Telecommunications (UPT)—are currently active, working together to pursue the vision of universal personal communications. The present and future wireless network systems currently known are summarized in Figure 11.1. The following subsections briefly describe some of the current research activities for future mobile systems and give us a flavor of what to expect in the future.

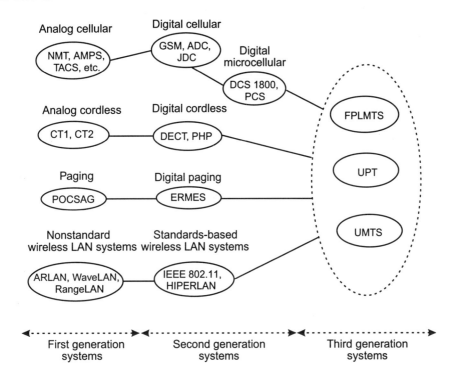

FIGURE 11.1   Wireless network systems to date.

11.4.1   The Universal Mobile Telecommunications System

The UMTS is a project (initiated by ETSI) in Europe under the RACE program [9]. The goal of UMTS is to be a universal multi-operator, multiservice digital system, building on the existing second-generation digital systems.

UMTS will provide support for existing mobile services and fixed telecommunication (ISDN and B-ISDN) services up to 2 Mbps or more, including high-speed data transmission, database retrieval, fax, video telephony, and high-quality voice telephony. UMTS will also support unique mobile services such as navigation, vehicle location, and road traffic information services. In addition, UMTS seeks to provide for low-cost PCS mobile terminals that support voice, data, and advanced video services and can be used anywhere (at home; in the office; or in public, rural, and urban centers) and everywhere (interoperator roaming).

To accomplish this futuristic goal, several projects within the RACE UMTS program are underway: air-interface requirements are being investigated through the Advanced TDMA (ATDMA) and the Code-Division Multiple Access Testbed (CODIT) projects [10–12]; mobility management and roaming issues are being explored through the Mobile Network (MONET) [13]; advanced radio planning tools are being explored through Planning Tools For Third-Generation Mobile Networks (PLATON) [14]; the development of future mobile audio visual terminals is being explored through MAVT [6]; and the development of mobile broadband systems (MBS) [15] supporting data transmission rates up to 100 Mbps is being explored to bridge the gap between UMTS and B-ISDN.

11.4.2 Universal Personal Telecommunications

In its vision to provide for universal personal telecommunications, the UPT provides access to telecommunications services while allowing personal mobility. Supported by the ITU-R (ITU-Radiocommunications, formerly CCITT), it enables a user to initiate and receive calls on the basis of a personal telecommunication number across multiple networks at any terminal, fixed or mobile, irrespective of geographic location. The idea behind UPT is that a user may register to receive incoming calls and originate outgoing calls at any terminal. If the UPT user is registered at a particular terminal, then outgoing calls can be made without user authentication or identification. As long as there are no restrictions on the user profile, the outgoing calls can be made and billed to the UPT user. On receiving an incoming call, the user is able to receive on the registered terminal [16,17].

In contrast to UMTS, which provides terminal mobility, UPT supports personal mobility, as services can be mapped to a user regardless of the terminal type (personal portable, mobile, or fixed terminals) and geographic location. The provides enormous flexibility to the user.

11.4.3 Future Public Land Mobile Telecommunications Systems (FPLMTS)

FPLMTS was originally initiated by the CCIR Task Group 8/1 (now ITU-R), and its main objective is to provide a range of services, such as voice, facsimile and data, on a worldwide basis, to be introduced in the year 2000. In addition, FPLMTS will provide voice and nonvoice services to users over a wide range of user densities and geographical coverage areas, including international roaming through land mobile and satellite communications [18].The services expected with FPLMTS can be categorized into six main information types—voice, audio, text, image, video, and signaling—covering such services as interactive, store and forward, broadcasting/narrowcasting, one-way/two-way messaging, and information retrieval [19]. Tables 11.1 and 11.2 give a hint of some of the applications expected.

The services envisioned for FPLMTS can be split into two broad categories— voice-based and signaling information services, and data-based information services. With the former, subscribers will be able to access a wide range of voice services such as voice messaging and speech retrieval, which allows users to access menu-based information services such as the weather, flight/travel information, shopping, and tourist information. With signaling applications, services that can be offered include telemetering (data acquisition, remote control, etc.) and caller number ID screening (or calling-party identification), where users are able to view the number of the caller before answering. The data services offer a richer set of services catered for the mobile data mass market. From e-mail to short messaging and paging, users with text-based wireless data terminals are able to access bulletin board information, city information, or electronic yellow pages. Image-based services will be able to provide fax messaging services with store-and-forward (mailbox) capabilities. Terminals with sketch pads will be able to send out faxes with drawings or sketches, such as street directions. In addition, as mentioned in Section 11.2, we can expect mobile navigation services, which will apply not only to vehicle, but to hikers and travelers as well.

Together with video-type services, teleshopping can be made available to the mobile data terminals by accessing catalogs, product ranges, etc. Video-based services will also support video telephony, video mail, and video-based information services such as city information, real estate, hotels, and holiday resorts.

TABLE 11.1

Typical FPLMTS Services: Voice, Audio, and Signaling

Type of Information	Service	Application	Data Rate
Voice	End-to-end voice connection	Two person/conference call	8–64 Kbps
	Store-and-forward voice	Voice mail box	8–64 Kbps
	Voice messaging (broad/narrowcasting)	Public service announcements	8–64 Kbps

TABLE 11.1 (continued)

Type of Information	Service	Application	Data Rate
	Speech retrieval	Telephone access to voice menu and stored voice information services	8–64 Kbps
Audio	Audiotex	Program sound	64–384 Kbps
Signaling	User location	Service profile	8 Kbps
	End-to-end signaling communication	Remote control and status acquisition	Connectionless packet data
	Access to stored signaling	Polling of telemetering stations	8–64 Kbps
	Store and forward signaling	Caller number ID	8–64 Kbps

TABLE 11.2
Typical FPLMTS Services: Text, Image, and Video

Type of Information	Service	Application	Data Rate
Text	Text information	Location information	8 Kbps
	End-to-end data connection	Data conversation	8–64 Kbps
		Connectionless short messaging	8–64 Kbps
	Store and forward text	E-mail	100 bps–64 Kbps
	Text retrieval	Electronic bulletin board	8–64 Kbps
		City information	8–64 Kbps
	Text messaging	Paging	8–64 Kbps
Image	Mobile navigation	Image indicating location of user	N/A
	End-to-end image connection	Fax	8–64 Kbps
	Store-and-forward images	Fax mailbox	8–64 Kbps

Type of Information	Service	Application	Data Rate
	Access to stored images	Teleshopping and catalog shopping	8–64 Kbps
Video	End-to-end video connection	Two-way video telephony	64–1920 Kbps
	Store-and-forward video	Video mail	64–1920 Kbps
	Access to stored moving images	Teleshopping	64–1920 Kbps
	Video clip selection	Teleshopping	64–1920 Kbps

In the recent World Administrative Radio Conference (WARC) 1992 meeting, the subbands 1885–2025 and 2110–2200 MHz have been allocated for the terrestrial portion of FPLMTS, and 2010–2025 and 2185–2200 MHz have been allocated for a combination of satellite and terrestrial components. The terrestrial bands are expected to take effect in the year 2000, while the space components will be implemented in 2010.

The concept behind FPLMTS is simple, with four different radio air-interfaces, R1–R4, as shown in Figure 11.2. R1 represents the air interface between a mobile station (MS) and the base station (BS). R2 is the air interface between a portable/personal station (PS) and the communicating base station (CS). To avoid confusion, MSs are typically vehicle mounted and PSs are pocket-sized portables. The R3 air interface allows communication between the satellite and mobile Earth station (MES). Finally the R4 air interface is the signaling interface used for paging or alerting in case a call is terminated at an FPLMTS terminal.

There are two components to FPLMTS: satellite and terrestrial. Satellite components involve the communication of land mobile terminals with satellites or can even be used to bridge terrestrial components, which are the conventional land mobile radio networks. Various application scenarios can be envisaged. In the residential environment, PSs can communicate with a personal base station, which is linked to the fixed network via the R2 air interface, or with an external cell site (CS) for PSs, such as in the cordless local loop applications. In the office environment, PSs can have access to the PSTN/ISDN either through personal base stations or through CSs, which are linked to the exchange directly or via the main PBX. For MSs in vehicles, the connection is made via the R1 interface to base stations (BS), which are in turn linked to the mobile exchange. Pedestrians are able gain access to the fixed network via the R2 interface. In the rural environment, the small exchanges are connected to MSs, which are then radioed to the BS via R1, with their ranges extendible by repeaters (RP). Wide-area pagers (WP) can be reached via the pager base station communicating over the R4 interface. All CSs and BSs are either linked to

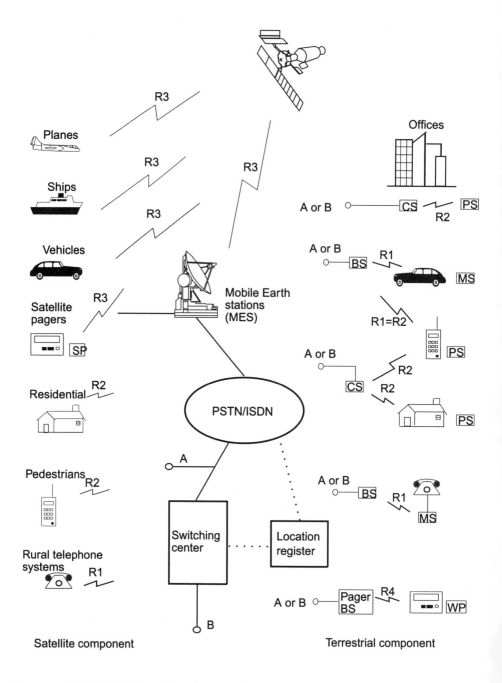

FIGURE 11.2 FPLMTS satellite and terrestrial components.

the PSTN/ISDN (A) or the switching center (B). The PSTN/ISDN and the switching centers have access to the location registers for identifying and registering the mobile users of the system. The terrestrial components can also have access to mobile satellite service (MSS), via the MES. Hence, if the fixed network is short of capacity, the MSS can be an alternative route.

For the satellite component, planes, ships, trains, and all other users can be connected to the MSS via the R3 interface. Pedestrian, residential and rural telephone systems users access the MES via their respective air interfaces and the fixed network. This gives users the added flexibility of being connected via satellite or terrestrial network, depending on the network loading. In addition, the service provides paging by satellite, whereby pagers can be reached via satellite (R3 interface) in any part of the world.

11.5 SATELLITE AND LAND MOBILE INTEGRATION

Without a doubt, the success of future personal telecommunications systems will depend very much on the integration of satellite and land mobile radio systems. Satellite systems are expected to complement terrestrial systems to provide rapid diffusion of services to the mass market. The advantage of a satellite component in a personal communication system, as in FPLMTS, is that it is able to support complete coverage for the deployment of terrestrial mobile systems, coverage extension to maritime and aeronautical users, and truly global roaming capabilities. Satellites are also able to provide an overlay of cells to existing micro and macro cells. Low Earth orbiting (LEO) satellites orbiting around 800 km above the Earth are able to form larger cells of several hundred kilometers in radius. At the WARC 92 conference, a worldwide frequency was allocated for LEO mobile satellite services, which consists of the bands from 1610 to 1626.5 MHz in the uplink (user to satellite) and 2483.5 to 2500 MHz in the downlink (satellite to user). To further overlay the larger cells, geostationary Earth orbit (GEO) satellites with multiple beams can form super cells.

Communication satellites can fit into future personal communications networks in several ways [20,21]. They can serve as international gateways, or they can provide direct personal connectivity. Satellite systems would also offer extended coverage to land mobile systems, so that when a user falls out of the terrestrial coverage area, the dual mode (with terrestrial and satellite transceivers) capabilities of the handset will communicate with the satellite component.

There are several existing or proposed satellite systems capable of offering personal communication services [22,23]. An ambitious project initiated by the International Maritime Satellite Organization (INMARSAT), known as Project 21, embarks on providing global telephone services by the year 2000. The services provided include high-quality voice, global roaming with a single number access, integral pager for standby call alerting, inbuilt position determination, and fax and data-handling capabilities. Another project launched by Motorola, the Iridium, is scheduled for operation in 1997. This system was to have been supported by 77 LEO satellites (Iridium has atomic number 77) but now the plans are to provide the same coverage with 66 satellites. These will give global coverage of voice and data for handheld terminals, with intersatellite connectivity and onboard switching. Globalstar is another system, formed by Loral Aerospace and Qualcomm to develop a system with a constellation of 48 LEO satellites for worldwide coverage. Globalstar is scheduled to be commissioned in 1996, providing voice, data, fax, interconnection with the PSTN, the public land mobile network (PLMN), and private networks, in addition to radio determination satellite services (RDSS). TRW [21] also has a system, known as the Odyssey, which will provide multiregional coverage with 12 satellites in medium-altitude orbits (MEO), and will use CDMA as the access technology. The Odyssey system will be compatible with terrestrial cellular systems—i.e., it will interoperate with GSM in Europe and IS-54 (American Digital Cellular) and AMPS in the U.S.

In addition, there is the extremely high-frequency land mobile satellite (ELMSAT) system, which has been proposed by the University of Rome to increase the capacity of GSM. The system is also expected to integrate terrestrial, maritime, and aeronautical users in the same network, provide high data rate services, and support ISDN-compatible services. Hence, we can expect to see several satellite systems that support FPLMTS's vision for a global satellite personal communications system.

11.6 CONCLUSIONS

The future of mobile data communications promises to be an exciting one offering a wide range of data services for the mass market. As with the vision of personal communications services, mobile data will be an integral part of everyone's lives. The infrastructure created by FPLMTS, UMTS, and UPT will be a platform to bring us into 21st-century mobile communications. Building on this, more innovative services and applications will no doubt promise us an exciting future ahead.

References

[1]   Carse, D., and G. Garrard, "A Continental Drift Towards Wireless Data," *Data Communications*, March 21, 1994, pp. 68–74.

[2]   Steele, R., and J.E.B. Williams, "Third Generation PCN and the Intelligent Multimode Mobile Portable," *IEE Electronic and Communication Engineering Journal*, Vol. 5, No. 3, London, June 1993, pp. 147–156.

[3]   Franzo, R., "The Key to Personal Communications," *Electronic Design*, Nov. 22, 1993, pp. 102.

[4]   Stedman, R., R. Steel, H. Gharavi, and L. Hanzo, "A 22 Kbd Mobile Video Telephone Scheme," *Proc. IEEE Vehicular Technology Conference*, Denver, CO, 1992, pp. 251–254.

[5]   Vaisey, J., E. Yuen, and J. Cavers, "Video Coding for Very High Bit Rate Mobile Data Transmission," *Proc. IEEE Vehicular Technology Conference*, Denver, CO, 1992, pp. 259–262.

[6]   Lappe, D., "Mobile Audio Visual Terminal (MAVT)," *Proc. Second International Conference on Universal Personal Communications*, ICUPC, Ottawa, Canada, Oct. 12–15, 1993, pp. 556–559.

[7]   Daly, P., "Navstar GPS and GLONASS: Global Satellite Navigation Systems," *IEE Electronic and Communication Engineering Journal*, Dec. 1993, pp. 349–357.

[8]   Catling I., Editor, *Advanced Technology for Road Transport: IVHS and ATT*, Norwood, MA: Artech House, 1994.

[9]   Commission of the European Communities, "Research and Technology Development in Advanced Communication Technologies in Europe," *Research for Advanced Communications in Europe Annual Report*, DG XIII, Brussels, 1993.

[10] Urie, A., "Advanced TDMA Mobile Access," *Proc. Second International Conference on Universal Personal Communications*, ICUPC, Ottawa, Canada, Oct. 12–15, 1993, pp. 392–396.

[11] Andermo, P.G., and G. Larsson, "Code Division Testbed, CODIT", *Proc. Second International Conference on Universal Personal Communications*, ICUPC, Ottawa, Canada, Oct. 12–15, 1993, pp. 397–401.

[12] "Special Issue on RACE Mobile Communications," *IEE Electronic and Communication Engineering Journal*, Vol. 5, No. 3, June 1993.

[13] Buitenwerf, E., and H. de Boer, "RACE MONET: Mobile Networks for UMTS," *Proc. Second International Conference on Universal Personal Communications*, ICUPC, Ottawa, Canada, Oct. 12–15, 1993, pp. 381–386.

[14] Esposito, C., and C. Willard, "PLATON," *Proc. Second International Conference on Universal Personal Communications*, ICUPC, Ottawa, Canada, Oct. 12–15, 1993, pp. 387–391.

[15] Chelouche, M., and A. Plattner, "Mobile Broadband Systems (MBS): Trends and Impact on 60 GHz Band MMIC Development," *IEE Electronic and Communication Engineering Journal*, June 1993, pp. 187–197.

[16] Cameron, R., "UPT Implementation in a CS1 Network Environment," *Proc. Second International Conference on Universal Personal Communications*, ICUPC, Ottawa, Canada, Oct. 12–15, 1993, pp. 103–107.

[17] Gort, J.E., and A.J. Gort, "A Planning Tool in Support of Network Signalling and Mobility Management for Universal Personal Telecommunications," *Proc. Second International Conference on Universal Personal Communications*, ICUPC, Ottawa, Canada, Oct. 12–15, 1993, pp. 93–97.

[18] Fudge, R., "FPLMTS Satellite Component—Service Roles," *Proc. Second International Conference on Universal Personal Communications*, ICUPC, Ottawa, Canada, Oct. 12–15, 1993, pp. 849–853.

[19] CCIR IWP 8/13, "FPLMTS," IWP 8/13-45, (COST 231 TD(89)049), Hakone, Japan, May 25–June 8, 1989.

[20] Kipreos, T., "Satellites and PCS: The Hybrid Approach," *Proc. Second International Conference on Universal Personal Communications*, ICUPC, Ottawa, Canada, Oct. 12–15, 1993, pp. 334–338.

[21] Horstein, M., "Odyssey—A Satellite-Based Personal Communications System," *Proc. Second International Conference on Universal Personal Communications*, ICUPC, Ottawa, Canada, Oct. 12–15, 1993, pp. 291–298.

[22] Ward, J.W., "Microsatellites for Global Electronic Mail Networks," *IEE Electronics and Communications Engineering Journal*, December 1991, pp. 267–272.

[23] Hughes, C.D., O. Koudelka, C. Garrido, M. Tomlinson, and J. Horle, "A Microterminal Satellite Data Communication System," *IEE Electronics and Communications Engineering Journal*, December 1991, pp. 243–251.

▼▼▼

GLOSSARY

A

ABM   asynchronous balanced mode (of data exchange)
ACK   positive acknowledgment
ADM   asynchronous disconnected mode (of data exchange)
ADF   average duration of a fade
ARQ   automatic repeat requests
ASK   amplitude shift keying

B

BER   bit error rate
BMA   Berlekamp-Massey Algorithm
BPF   band pass filter
bps   bits per second
BPSK   binary phase shift keying

C

CB   coherence bandwidth
CDLC   cellular data link control
CDMA   code-division multiple access

CDPD	cellular digital packet data
CPM	continuous phase modulation
CT	coherence time
CTS	clear to send
CRC	cyclic redundancy check
CSMA	carrier sense multiple access

D

DECT	digital European cordless telecommunications
DSB-SC-AM	double sideband suppressed carrier amplitude modulation
DSMA	digital sense multiple access

E

ETSI	European Telecommunications Standards Institute

F

FDMA	frequency-division multiple access
FEC	forward error correction
FFSK	fast frequency shift keying
FM	frequency modulation
FSK	frequency shift keying

G

GBN	go back N (an ARQ protocol)
GM	group mode (of data exchange)
GMSK	Gaussian minimum shift keying
GPS	global positioning system
GSM	global system for mobile communications

H

HDB	home database
HDLC	high-level data-link control

I

ISI	intersymbol interference

J

JDC	Japanese digital cellular system

K

Kbps	kilobits per second

L

LOS	line of sight
LPF	low pass filter

M

MAC	media access control
Mbps	megabits per second
MDBS	mobile data base station
M-ES	mobile-end system
MD-IS	mobile data intermediate system
MSK	minimum shift keying
MST	multiple segment transactions

N

NADC	North American digital cellular
NAK	negative acknowledgment

O

OSI	open systems interconnection

P

PARS	private advanced radio system
PDA	personal digital assistant
PDF	probability density function
PDO	packet data optimized
PHP	personal handy phone
PIM	personal information manager
PLL	phase locked loop
PM	phase modulation
POCSAG	Post Office Code Standardization Advisory Group
PSK	phase shift keying

Q

QAM	quadrature amplitude modulation
QPSK	quadrature phase shift keying

R

RACE	Research for Advanced Communications in Europe
RTS	request to send

S

SAW	stop and wait (an ARQ protocol)
SR	selective repeat (an ARQ protocol)
SSC	selective signaling code
SST	single segment transactions

T

TDMA	time-division multiple access
TETRA	trans-European trunked radio

U

UADG	User Access Definition Group

V

VCO	voltage-controlled oscillator
VDB	visitor database

▼▼▼

ABOUT THE AUTHORS

Peter Wong graduated with Bachelors and Masters degrees in electrical engineering from the University College of Swansea, U.K. He majored in mobile data communications systems and has research interests in propagation, error control, and mobility management. He has served as a research fellow and held similar positions at British Telecom Laboratories, investigating various aspects of mobile communications. In Europe, he participated as an expert in the European Union project COST 231, "Digital Land Mobile Radio Communications" and has presented his research work in various international conferences. He has also been a research engineer at the Hong Kong Telecom Institute of Information Technology, investigating many aspects of mobile communications, such as error control and dynamic channel allocation for cellular systems. At present he is the regional technical manager for AT&T Asia Pacific. Based in Hong Kong, he is responsible for the design of mobile communications networks (cellular voice and data) in the Asia Pacific Region.

David Britland has spent some 30 years in radio engineering. At Motorola Storno, he was chief engineer for the U.K. systems engineering division, and he spent a period on secondment to ETSI in Nice, France, where he was involved in the writing of test methods for mobile radio type approval. Mr. Britland has expertise in PMR systems and products (including digital trunked radio), encryption, and cellular radio. He has also significant knowledge of wire line communications and was involved in digital facsimile research during the early 1970s. He is chairman of RES7, the ETSI committee specifying the standard for digital short range radio (DSRR). He is a member of the BSI Road Traffic Informatics committee EEL/37. He is principal consultant and technical director at RAM Communications Consultants Ltd.

▼▼▼

INDEX

The Artech House Telecommunications Library

Vinton G. Cerf, Series Editor

For further information on these and other Artech House titles, contact:

Artech House
685 Canton Street
Norwood, MA 02062
617-769-9750
Fax: 617-769-6334
Telex: 951-659
email: artech@world.std.com

Artech House
Portland House, Stag Place
London SW1E 5XA England
+44 (0) 171-973-8077
Fax: +44 (0) 171-630-0166
Telex: 951-659
email: bookco@artech.demon.co.uk